Your Vehicle for Business Success

Successful business made easy

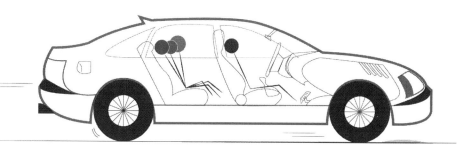

Moinuddin Nishar Ahmed Kolia

Author services by Pedernales Publishing, LLC
www.pedernalespublishing.com

Author's cover photograph by John Cassidy.

British Library Cataloguing in Publication Data.

A catalogue record for this book is available from the British Library.

Paperback edition   ISBN 978-1-499107-15-9

I dedicate this book to my amazing and outstanding Parents

Nishar Ahmed Ibrahim kolia and Najma Nishar Ahmed Kolia

Thank you for everything that you have done for me and especially for your support, confidence and trust that you have given me.

ACKNOWLEDGEMENTS

Firstly I want to acknowledge the inspiration that I received from my Creator that allowed me to come up with 'Your vehicle for business success' model whilst I sat in my lounge wondering about how I was going to explain business structure, business strategies and create a business framework to five business partners with whom I was about to begin a business venture.

I would also like to acknowledge those from whom I have learned so much. Their insights have influenced my business practice and a lot of what you will learn through my book. My Parents were my first teachers and in no particular order; Anthony Robbins, Keith Cunningham, Christopher Howard, Dr Joanna Martin, Daniel Wagner, James Watson, Dan Bradbury, Andy Harrington and Dan S Kennedy.

I also want to acknowledge Paul Cosens who has been a great friend and started me on my journey and Kevin Bermingham for helping me to get this book out of my head and into my hands.

I'd like to acknowledge the lessons that I have received from all the people that I have had the privilege of working with in my businesses, all of my business partners and my friends that help me put my book together. I am very grateful for all your help, support and confidence that you have given me. Each one of you has been instrumental in my business journey. Thank-you.

CONTENTS

INTRODUCTION

What is a pharmacist doing writing a book on business? I mean you go to a pharmacist when you are ill but where do you go when your business is not feeling well?

I have a remedy for business illness and that is why I believe that this book is the perfect prescription for you, if you are looking to improve the health of your business.

In December 2010 I had decided to open a second branch of my pharmacy, Moin's Chemist and Wellbeing Centre in Market Harborough. In order for this to happen I needed to sign a 5-year lease, costing me £25k annually. Had this business failed to live up to my expectations then I would have ended up with a loss in excess of £250k as set up and running costs are very high.

In January 2012, I decided to take on five partners to join me on this journey. Of these five pharmacists, only one of them had previously owned his own business, which he had closed 15 years ago. All of the others were locums with very little business experience. The one thing that they did possess was a lot of passion and commitment.

I created this model 'your vehicle for business success,' so that they could understand and appreciate business as a whole and know what is involved in running it successfully.

THE VEHICLE

This is the framework that I used to teach my business partners the concept of business. The vehicle is a car and each component of the car represents an aspect of business. Many concepts in business can be difficult or complicated to understand or appreciate. However this model not only simplifies it, it also allows you to create your own business framework as you work through the exercises.

When you start thinking about all the things that are involved in running a business, let alone a successful one, it can be overwhelming. There are lots of things that will need your attention. The good news is that not all the things need to be tackled at the same time. So how do we prioritise which aspects of the business to focus on?

This book will show you how each aspect is prioritised and what you need to take into consideration when planning and running your business.

Starting a new business is easy

How can starting a new business be easy when one in three new start-up businesses close within the first year of trading and according to some statistics two in three start-ups are no longer in business after three years?

There are many reasons why businesses fail; it could be that you were never totally passionate about your business or that you have lost that spark because the challenges in the business have been so overwhelming.

If you jump into your business with both feet first, it can cause a lack of clarity and purpose. The haste tends to mean that you may become too involved in working *in* the business rather than *on* the business. This can significantly increase your chances of failure due to the lack of planning and strategising. As Sir Winston Churchill said, 'If you fail to plan, you plan to fail.' This is true for your business and many business owners never plan.

Having a successful business is easy if you have discovered your passion for it and know that there is money to be made in it. This is covered in the first priority of the vehicle for your business success in chapter 3.

Planning and strategising your business is discussed in more detail in the second priority and chapter 4. This includes the need for Plan B, a contingency plan, which will provide a smoother and smarter transition from Plan A to Plan B if needed. All of which is necessary to enhance your chances of having a successful business.

The final piece in the jigsaw for a successful business is that you are able to pounce on all of the opportunities that come your way. That you focus on the direction of your business without really getting bogged down in all of the details. This is the third priority, which is covered in chapter 5.

The truth is that successful business owners know how to run their business. They have mastered the skills that are necessary to be winners. Once you have been through this book and completed the exercises in it, you will have an amazing insight into your business and will be equipped with all the tools that are needed to be successful.

Make the money that you want and deserve

Many business owners never make the money that they would like in their business or the money that their efforts deserve. Do you want to have a business that barely breaks even each year? If businesses made the money that their owners wanted and deserved then almost 70 per cent of businesses would not close within three years. Are you financially stable in your business? Are you making the money that you want? Are you able to provide for your family as you would like? If your answers to any of these questions is 'no', then you are not making the money that you want from your business.

I know many business owners that work very long hours, they would never work those hours if they were working for someone else and their take home pay is probably less than or the same as when they were in a job. In some cases when you calculate the hours worked and the money that they pay themselves, it works out to be less than half of what they would have earned in employment. When you are getting results like this then it is only a matter of time before your motivation for running your business starts to disappear.

In your business do you pay everyone else first before you pay yourself? If you are thinking of starting a business then do you want to pay everyone else first and then take home the loose change that is left?

If you have been on a plane, and I'm pretty sure most of you have, you will know the emergency drill they go through before each flight. The rule is to help yourself first when the oxygen masks come down. Why? Well without helping yourself first you are at a greater risk of passing out. If you pass out then you will not be able to help anybody, not even your loved ones. This same rule applies to your business. If your survival cannot be guaranteed then all those that depend on you will also suffer.

I know that I would like to be paid first in my business but this does not mean that I pay myself first at the expense of others. It means that I should establish a business that can create enough wealth to pay me and take care of all those that are around me.

You can do this if you have first carried out a viability check on your business and then identify many of the income streams. This allows you to understand the financial mechanics of your business and once you know where the money is coming from all you have to do is go there and fill up. You can only drive to the filling station if you know what it is that you are looking for and know how to get there.

Get the life that you want

Do you know of any business owners that are so involved in their business that it takes over their life? Often this happens because there is a lack of clarity in their life and especially in their business. Time overtakes them and as they get drawn more and more to working in their business, they get too busy to have time to do anything else. If you are not careful this can happen to you. Then it soon starts to seem that life is passing you by and as each day comes and goes there is more and more frustration. There is a feeling of being trapped and you cannot see where your life and business is heading. If you are a parent, it could mean that before you even realise it, all of your children have grown up and you have been absent from their lives. When you are hit with this realisation it could create a feeling of resentment towards you and perhaps your business too.

How do you expect your business to grow and be a success when you are feeling overwhelmed, frustrated, angry and resentful towards it? These emotions and feelings then play out in your life. Is that the life that you had always dreamed about?

Your business should be a platform for creating the life that you want. It should be something that you are proud of building. It becomes the reason why you have had a life of abundance and fulfilment.

This is possible in your business and it is easy to achieve this. Successful business people will visualise what they want. They have clarity for what they want for their business and their life. They have planned and strategised the direction for their business and are well prepared or willing to be innovative when faced with adversaries and challenges. They direct their energies towards achieving their goals and this creates momentum for more success in their business. They are passionate and motivated by their business and it gives them a lot of pleasure going into the business to work. You become part of the gratitude cycle, success breeds more success and that gives you fulfilment and a sense of purpose that allows you to have a lot of gratitude for what you have. You truly can have the life that you want when you have a successful business and this is easy.

MY JOURNEY

Having graduated as a pharmacist in 1993 from Liverpool School of Pharmacy, I went to an independent pharmacy group to do my pre-registration training and got on the register of the Royal Pharmaceutical Society as a pharmacist in 1994. For the first year of my life as a pharmacist, I worked as a locum pharmacist working mostly in the Midlands. This gave me the opportunity to see how many of my colleagues and the large chain of pharmacies operated and ran their business. In 1995 I started working as a pharmacist manager for an independent pharmacy that was a 10-minute walk from my home. In October 1998 I got my big break and bought the business, which I had by now been managing for the past three years. I bought that business when it had a turnover of £244k and in the financial year end March 2013 we posted a turnover of £1.6m in that business alone. Also our second branch is expected to have a turnover of almost £400k in our first year of trading. I have started to export medicines to the Middle East and Africa and I am in the process of successfully establishing my Internet pharmacy business. I reveal this to you not to impress you but to impress *upon* you all of the possibilities that are out there.

HOW WAS ALL OF THIS POSSIBLE?

When I graduated as a pharmacist, I was always very passionate about my profession. If there was any situations that needed medical assistants, I would be the first one there declaring loudly that I am a pharmacist. In fact I was so passionate about it that my siblings used to joke, 'here comes the pharmacist', at every opportunity. When I remember and think of those days, it still brings a smile to my face. I loved being a pharmacist so passion was not an issue.

In my pharmacy I saw many patients that had come with an illness, like diabetes or high blood pressure and many of them would then see the list of their medicines grow, despite which their ailments would continue to get worse. Their health and medication was being very poorly managed. Then as time went on I noticed that other members of the same family were now being diagnosed with similar diseases. This led me to believe that there needed to be better health education, enabling families to manage their health in a more holistic manner. This would involve health screening, education and greater choices in treatments by having complimentary therapies available from the pharmacy. I wanted to be at the heart of the community for health matters and issues. This became our values and the vision for the pharmacy.

The business had been growing year on year and we had reached a point where further growth had become impossible because our premises and facilities would not allow it. The shop that we had been working in was a very narrow and long pharmacy and only had one floor. The shop next door also belonged to the same landlord and this was almost twice as wide as our own shop.

I toyed with the possibility of taking over the shop next door. There were three issues that needed to be dealt with. One, although the shop had the potential to be as long as my present property, the fire exit from my pharmacy ran behind about half of the shop area of the premises next door. Hence the shop next door was twice as wide but only half as long. Two, it was occupied and three, the cost.

I worked out what it would cost me to rent the premises next door and then extrapolated it to establish the fixed cost of the project. I did this using the figures that I had from my existing business and then applying them in the new business. This obviously was not the exact figures but a very good estimate. I analysed the business as it was. I looked at the worst-case scenario first. If we had no extra income in the business from the new facilities then could I afford to pay all of my expenses? The answer was pretty much yes. I then looked at the potential for the extra income in the business. This allowed me to understand that there was a great chance that this business model would work. Now I just needed to work out how much it would cost to put the plan in to action and create a cash flow projection.

The project was estimated to cost around £500k to complete. This involved demolishing both buildings, my premises from which I was trading and the premises next door that I was considering to rent. Whilst the work would be undertaken, I would have to trade from a building in the side street around the corner from the original business site. I assumed that we would lose about 33 per cent of business due to the disruption caused by the building works. A cash flow projection was calculated and I also worked out how much extra money I would need to raise and when I would need it. I then figured out when I was likely to be able to pay back the investors from whom I was going to raise the balance for the funds in this project.

After determining that the project was viable and calculating the cash flow projections, my next step was to plan how I was going to make it all happen. I had to persuade the present tenants to vacate the premises and then convince the landlord that I had the funds and the know-how to demolish two of his buildings and rebuild them again. These are just two of many challenges that we would encounter on this journey. I listed all the milestones that needed to be met. I knew my weaknesses, and as one of them was paying attention to detail I delegated much of this element to a very good   practice manager that I had recently employed. We planned in detail all things that we needed to do to reach each milestone. We got the ball rolling and the building work began in September 2008 and we were open for business in our newly built premises on 1st July 2009. During the process we assessed our staffing levels and skilled up those that needed to be so that we could be ready to deliver new services from these facilities. We had the pharmacy designed to reflect our branding and image. I also knew that the newly built facilities would have us streets ahead of our competition.

As it happened the disruptions from the building work had little impact on business and within four years of rebuilding the pharmacy we had more than doubled the business. Yet the potential for growth within the pharmacy is still huge. Success breeds success and so there have been many other added benefits, including the establishing of our second branch, the wholesaling and the Internet pharmacy.

The business has continued to grow steadily and I have been tweaking things as I have seen fit. I have been using skills and tools that I have learnt to make the business even more efficient and profitable. This is the exact process that I had used in growing a £244k business that today is generating £1.6m and creating several other business ventures that I may not have had had this step not been taken.

WHAT'S IN IT FOR YOU?

I have been harping on about my achievements and how I have been so successful in my business. So how will this book benefit you?

It is easy to have a successful business once you understand it.

You too can have a successful business easily

Once you understand the principles of business and know how to apply them you can also have a successful and a thriving business. In this book you will learn and understand all of the concepts of business through my analogy of a vehicle – in this case a car. This simplifies a lot of the complicated aspects of business and understanding of the concepts will be made significantly easier by allowing you to appreciate how each concept fits in with another.

You will gain knowledge as to why that concept is important, what it is and how you can apply it into your business. As you apply each step, you will be making progress in building a strong business. By going through this book it is possible for you to build your business from concept to success

Vision, clarity and strategy for your business

Through the exercises you will discover and establish a vision for your business. This vision in turn will help you create focus and drive for success. When you have a vision, you can steer your business towards it. Your business will not feel like a burden but a pleasure.

Once you have set yourself an objective you can go out there and achieve it but if you are unclear about where you are going then where you will end up? When your vision becomes a reality in your business, you will have the business that you have worked for and wanted. This will also give you the life that you had wanted because your vision is built around the things that you value. There is a sense of achievement and fulfilment because your striving has been worth it. This will also become the pedestal for future achievement because success breeds success. You will be well and truly on the gratitude cycle.

Upon completing the exercises in the first priority detailed in chapter 3, you will start to gain clarity in your business. This will allow you to create momentum and drive as you now have the direction to where your business needs to go. There is a form of confidence that appears when you have clarity about anything in life and this is no different with your business. When you have clarity you know what it is that you want so it is simply a matter of planning the journey to get to where you want to be.

As you start to tackle the exercises in the second priority you start the planning process. This is done in two stages, the milestone markers and the detailed steps for each milestone. This will allow you to plan each stage and situation in your business. You can strategise it to such a level that you will be able to nominate somebody else to carry out the steps and you will still have the ability to reach your goal provided you have been following the progress that is being made in your business.

You will discover your vision, gain clarity and have a strategy to create and build a successful and a well maintained business.

Discover novel ways to grow your business

You will discover novel ways to grow your business. You will gain knowledge of how you can make the most of the people you know and how they can support you when you are going through a difficult time and feeling stuck. This network can also help you make faster progress when things are good.

There are lots of expert ideas for growing your business, from discovering your ideal customer and how to find them, to looking at your business closely for clues that will accelerate the profit. This includes things like looking at your daily figures, reducing the money lost in your business due to unnecessary expenses and making sure that you have received the correct amount of money that you should have from the goods that you have sold or from the services that you have provided. You will learn tools that will help your business run efficiently, like a well-oiled engine in a car.

Making the most of your life

Do you go to work or run a business as a hobby or is there a bigger purpose? Are you in your business because you are making a living out of it? This is important but also you want to ensure that you do not become a slave to your business. This means that you must create time for yourself and for the ones that you love and for the things that really matter to you in life. Your business is a means for you to do that. When this is achieved then you know that your efforts in your business have been worthwhile. Your business should give you the wealth, time and the life that you deserve. When this becomes part of your vision then this is what you will strive for. When your business starts to deliver your goals, it inspires you to set your standards even higher, which will create more wealth and you can use this to create more time for yourself and do the things that you want in life. You will only do this if it is part of your vision and your aim is to get to that position quickly otherwise you will forever be stuck in the rat race. Many business owners become so overwhelmed and are sucked into the system that they do not have the time to even assess how well their business is doing. Whatever you focus on grows and if you are consciously focusing on creating time for yourself and your family then that will happen. This can be done when you set your vision and strategy for your business which is what you will do as you go through this book. If you utilise the tools that you learn from this book, you will surely have the life, time and wealth that you have planned for, deserve and want.

HOW TO GET THE MOST OUT OF THIS BOOK AND YOUR BUSINESS

This book provides you with solutions for running your business successfully and so it is important that you complete the exercises in the order they appear. Before the exercises begin, read the vehicle analogy in chapter 2. This will give you the grounding and understanding of business concepts and will help you focus when you come to doing the exercises.

CASE STUDIES

You can download case studies from our website:
www.yourvehicleforbusinesssuccess.com

The case studies are based around real businesses that have used the 'your vehicle for business success' model to strategise their business. These case studies will help your understanding of the exercises, what is involved in doing them and appreciate the outcomes that were achieved.

They will give you faith and trust in the exercises and therefore greater confidence in your business once you have completed them.

DOWNLOAD THE TOOL 'YOUR VEHICLE FOR BUSINESS SUCCESS'

You can download the model of 'your vehicle for business success' and fill in the relevant exercises in their appropriate areas of the model.

The exercises will help you create the framework for your business and completing it on the download of the model will help you keep the information organised and in one place. This will allow you to have access to the information that you want, when you want it. You will not need to trawl through books to find what it is that you are looking for. This is very useful as all your notes will be very organised and well kept. You can keep adding to it, without having to find new pages.

Ideas can come at some of the craziest moments and when you come up with them you need to write them down on something. You can easily add these notes into the programme, hence there is no need to have lots of bits of paper hanging around. Scrap papers can also be lost easily which could result in losing what may have been very vital and valuable information.

Download the model to create the blueprint for your successful business now on *www.yourvehicleforbusinesssuccess.com*.

SUMMARY AND KEY LEARNING

Having a successful business is easy provided we understand what is required to make it happen. This can be summarised in the following way.

Having a viable business

It is extremely important that your business is viable. Have you ever come up with an idea that seems absolutely amazing and to you it feels like it is the best thing since sliced bread but no one else agrees with you? Many people have a great idea for business yet their customers do not always agree. We know this because more than two out of three businesses do not survive for more than three years. You do not want to be part of that statistic. You must ensure that your business is based on solid projection and strategy. When you are involved in a business that is not viable it creates anxiety, frustration and anger.

When you have established a well-orchestrated and viable business, you have the potential to create an amazing life for yourself and for those that you love. This is why it is important that you determine the viability of your existing business model before committing to it.

Having a vision for your business

Having a vision gives you something to aim for. When you have no vision for your business then you are leaving your business to chance. When you fire an arrow but you have no target, where will your arrow end up? When you have a vision for your business, you should also take into consideration the life that you want to live so that you can then strategies for that. When you have a vision that you share with your team it creates a momentum and drive within your organisation. This will generate excitement and something for the team to focus on and look forward to. Having a vision for your business is crucial for success because this is setting the destination for where you want to be in your business over time. When you attain and achieve the goals that you have set out, you will recognise it and appreciate the journey you have made and the people that have supported you towards that success. When you have a vision you get to it sooner because there is clarity and a purpose for your business. So begins the gratitude cycle.

Your strategy for business success

How many people do you know that talk the talk and walk the walk? There are many people that have a lot to say but very little to show for it. It is all very well to know that you have a viable business and a great vision for it too but if you are not going to strategise to make it happen, then it will always remain a beautiful dream.

Your strategy will give you the guidance and steps to follow to fulfil your vision for your life and your business. In turn this will also give you the confidence to know that your dream can come true. Having a strategy will allow you to make progress towards your goal, it will keep you focused and on track for achieving success in your business. When your strategy works for you, your business can truly make your dreams come true.

The time for action is now

It is great to have a viable business, great vision and go through the process of having a strategy that will realise your business success but nothing will happen unless you take action. This book will give you great tools to create an outstanding business for you that will have the potential to give you the life that you have been dreaming about. It is only a matter of time before it comes true, all you now have to do is make it happen. So let us get started.

BROWSE BEFORE YOU BUY

WHY DO I NEED TO KNOW THE VEHICLE?

Business Plan is not enough.

One in three new businesses fail in the first year. Many new businesses are started with the use of borrowed money. The most common sources for this are the banks. For this the business owner needs to demonstrate that their business will be profitable and viable with the submission of a business plan. The banks (or any other lender) would never entertain any notion of funding until they are satisfied with the plan. Why is it then that so many businesses fail despite new owners providing a business plan and hopefully writing out their strategy?

They fail because a business plan is a simple setting out of profit and loss accounts, this means that the plan only takes into account how much money they expect to come in and how much expense they have estimated to occur. It fails to take into consideration many of the factors that are necessary to run a successful business. Also many people simply exaggerate their plan in order to get the finances they need. The plan is then never given any more thought and fails to deliver anything more than acquiring the funds.

This framework is much more than a business plan. It is your framework for running a successful business. It will help you plan, strategise, execute and grow your business.

Overcome the overwhelm

Running a business is not simply about buying a commodity at one price and selling it for more than you bought it for. There are many things that need to be taken into consideration, which can overwhelm both newbie and existing business owners.

I want to help you to overcome being overwhelmed in your business and help you to prioritise effectively to be successful simply by implementing 'your vehicle for business success.'

Discover your passion.

Many people go into business because they believe that they want to make a living out of it. Yet they have no experience, love or connection to the business that they are starting.

If you do not love or value what you are doing, then the chances of success is small. If every day becomes a chore then your results will reflect that.

If you had a job then by the end of the week or month you would take home a salary. You are not always guaranteed a wage when you start out in business. Many business owners work harder, longer and for less pay than they would if they were employed.

Do you have the passion and the will to keep going when the going gets tough? The vehicle will help you discover your passion for the business that you are thinking of going into.

I already have the passion

Great – many people are very passionate about things in their life e.g. sport, cooking, travelling, clothes etc. and they want to turn their passion into a business.

These people will have a lot of energy, drive and passion for their business but if they have not thought things through then they may find that their passion and love for things is not making them any money. This can be very demotivating and demoralising.

The vehicle will help you to address issues such as how will I make my money, what are my expenses and cash flow issues? It will allow you to appreciate the intricacies of your chosen business and help you decide whether it is financially viable.

Hidden resources

Many of us want to do things all by ourselves. We are embarrassed to ask others for help. Sometimes we need help but we are scared of even addressing the matter. How often have our friends asked for help and we have gone out of our way to go and support them? What is even more surprising is that we would probably help people we hardly know, even strangers, especially if they paid us, if only they ask. So why do we believe that we cannot take advantage of that same goodwill?

The vehicle will help you identify how you can get the most from your network, your business partners and your customers.

Chemistry between the business partners

Too often businesses fail because somewhere along the line there is some sort of a rift or differences between the business partners.

If these could be identified at the outset of your business then the chances of the business being destroyed by misunderstanding will be less likely.

The vehicle will help optimise relationships between business partners.

Drill in the basics

Too often we take the basics for granted and we then start to ignore them. If our foundation is weak and our appreciation for the importance of the basics is poor then the chances for our success is limited.

The vehicle will help you understand and appreciate the basics so that you can build a firm foundation for future success.

Growing your team

Your team and staff are probably the most important element of your business. They are an investment, a necessity for growth and they are more valuable than your customers. As you are building your team, it essential that the people you employ fit into your systems and become an integral part of the business.

The vehicle will help you identify when you need to employ staff and what qualities each person would have to have to be a member of your team.

Innovation

Often we see that a business idea is doing well or we have a good business idea, yet when we try to copy them, we may not get the desired results. However, if we are able to plan and integrate innovations into our business, we can create a unique positioning that will help us be different from our competitors.

The vehicle will inspire innovation and help integrate it into your business.

THE VEHICLE

The vehicle is a car and the different parts of that car represent an aspect of business. Certain concepts in business can be difficult to understand or appreciate fully in their own right. However we can utilise an analogy that everyone understands to build a link between the two and so have a more thorough appreciation for their business and what is involved in having a successful one.

Two years ago (Jan 2011), I had invited 20 pharmacists to a presentation that I was doing. During this presentation they were offered an opportunity to join me in partnership in a business venture that I wanted to undertake. I was looking for three more partners, I had already taken on two other partners, to invest £25K each into the project of establishing a new pharmacy on the outskirts of Leicester. Our competition was three of the biggest pharmacy outlets in the UK and one independent pharmacy that has been established by the proprietor since 1977.

Of the 20, seven showed an interest from which we, my two partners and I, chose the three partners whom we had decided would be best for our business. These new partners had no business skills; the first had worked for a multiple for several years as a relief pharmacist manager. The second, although qualified since 1996 had only ever worked as a locum pharmacist (similar to being a supply teacher) while the third had only qualified the year before and had worked as a locum since then. They did not know each other prior to coming to the presentation.

How did I take three pharmacists with no business skills and create a business that has a turnover of more than £400k in a year?

First, I had to teach them the appreciation of business. This had to be done without jargon and in a manner that they could easily understand and apply. Hence, I came up with 'your vehicle for business success,' in order to develop their insight and business knowledge.

HOW DO YOU DRIVE THIS VEHICLE?

This section will introduce you to the vehicle. The vehicle that I want you to think about is a car. Everyone knows what a car is and how it works and here I have simply tried to highlight some of those qualities and create an analogy that can be used to understand each aspect of business.

The Driver – Business owner/s

The business owner is like the driver in the vehicle.

The driver is in control of the vehicle, they are responsible for the direction that the vehicle goes in, decides when to go up and down in gears, can steer the car towards wherever he or she wants to go, can choose to have a smooth ride or rough ride. They may decide to do something if the tyres go flat or they may keep driving.

The driver can enjoy being in control of the ride or allow themselves to be taken on a ride. The driver is in a very powerful position yet a very responsible one.

If the engine is making funny noises then the driver can choose to ignore it or do something about it. Whilst driving the vehicle the driver can either focus on the road ahead whilst occasionally glancing in the mirror, or decide to focus entirely on what's in the mirror.

If the fuel is running low then the driver can take their vehicle to the relevant petrol station and fill it with the appropriate fuel. If they notice that there is oil leaking from the engine, they can decide to tighten things up or just let it carry on.

The driver can choose what type of interiors they want or when to clean the windscreen. If the brakes became faulty the driver can either repair them or risk them failing by doing nothing about it. Should the brakes fail it could endanger the vehicle and more importantly the other passengers in the vehicle.

The driver can influence the nature of the journey with the passengers. He or she can make the journey very pleasant and everybody can have fun while on the journey or they can create a very difficult atmosphere and the whole ride can feel very uncomfortable and awkward.

If the journey is planned well then the experience can be fulfilling, exciting, challenging at times, yet very rewarding. If not, it can be the opposite.

The driver is like the business owner because the business owner needs to be motivated about their business, they need to ensure that the cash flow in their business is healthy and if there are challenges then they need to rise to them.

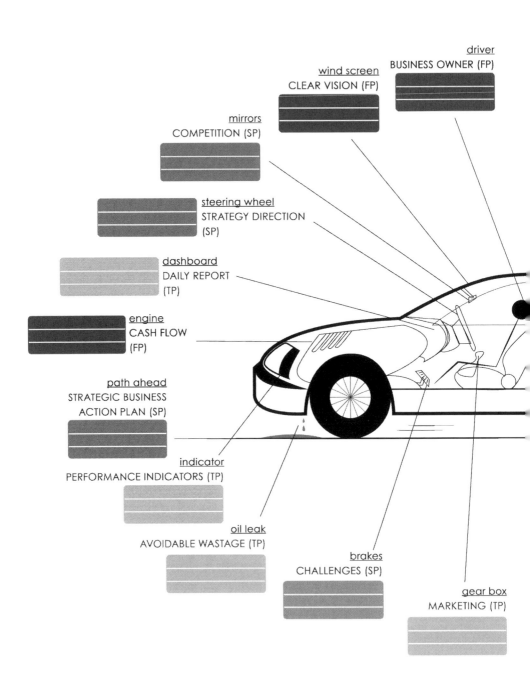

driver
BUSINESS OWNER (FP)

wind screen
CLEAR VISION (FP)

mirrors
COMPETITION (SP)

steering wheel
STRATEGY DIRECTION
(SP)

dashboard
DAILY REPORT
(TP)

engine
CASH FLOW
(FP)

path ahead
STRATEGIC BUSINESS
ACTION PLAN (SP)

indicator
PERFORMANCE INDICATORS (TP)

oil leak
AVOIDABLE WASTAGE (TP)

brakes
CHALLENGES (SP)

gear box
MARKETING (TP)

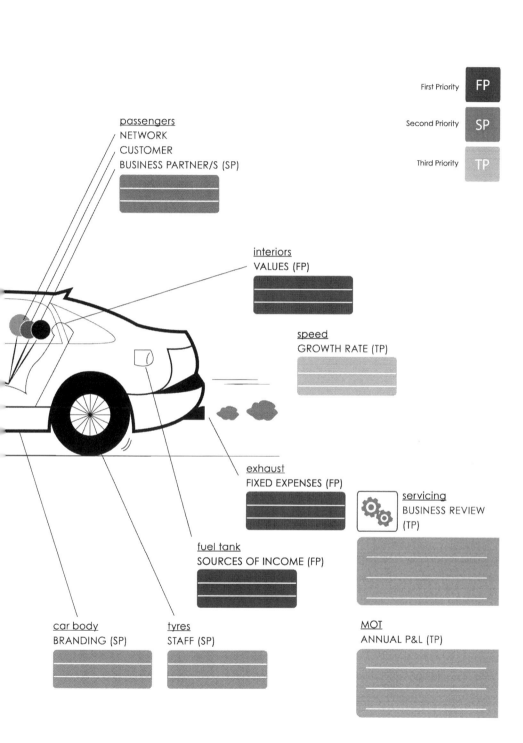

First Priority **FP**

Second Priority **SP**

Third Priority **TP**

passengers
NETWORK
CUSTOMER
BUSINESS PARTNER/S (SP)

interiors
VALUES (FP)

speed
GROWTH RATE (TP)

exhaust
FIXED EXPENSES (FP)

servicing
BUSINESS REVIEW
(TP)

fuel tank
SOURCES OF INCOME (FP)

car body
BRANDING (SP)

tyres
STAFF (SP)

MOT
ANNUAL P&L (TP)

Passengers – Your business partners, your customers and your network.

The passengers represent your business partners, your customers and your network.

These are the people that you will take on the journey with you. If your passengers are having a hard and difficult ride then it may not be long before they get out of the vehicle. If they enjoy the ride they will support you and make the trip fun. They can aid you in times of difficulty and encourage more people to want to join you on your journey. If the passengers in your vehicle are satisfied and happy you can expect a great journey ahead.

The passengers are like your business partners, your customers and your network because if your business does not meet the needs of this group of people they will leave, but if you please them they will help you grow.

The Interior – The owner's business values

The interior of your vehicle represent the business values.

The interior is reflective of the inner qualities of the car. Whether it is luxurious or not, does it have all the trimmings and the added extras?

The inside of the car can show someone how well looked after the vehicle is. If it is immaculate and pristine then all the passengers will appreciate it. If it is dirty or the seats are torn with litter everywhere then this leaves the passengers to make a judgement on the driver and on the car as well.

You can choose to look after the interior and maintain it, or let it run down. It is easy to make excuses but with if the interior is run down you can expect your journey to be uncomfortable.

The vehicle interior represents your business values and these are the things that are important to you in running your business. If all of your values are met then you will be happy and are likely to deliver a service that will be appreciated by your customers and will satisfy your partners.

The windscreen – Clear vision

The windscreen represents the vision for your business.

Imagine that the windscreen of your car is dirty and visibility through it is poor. Any looming hazards ahead may be missed which could have catastrophic effects on your vehicle, from being run off the road to being involved in a serious accident.

The passengers in the car will also lose confidence and may even bail out before things go horribly wrong.

A clear windscreen allows for a clearer visual assessment of the road ahead. Everyone knows exactly what direction the vehicle is heading in, there is an air of confidence and everybody will want to stay on board.

Occasionally, the windscreen can become dirty or steamed up but as long as that is being addressed, everyone will gladly continue to enjoy the ride.

The vision for your business is like the windscreen of your vehicle because it needs to be clear so that you can see it and get to it.

The engine – Cash flow

If the engine in your car blows up, then your vehicle will no longer be mobile. Your car has stopped working and there no further progress in your journey. Your vehicle is now useless as it is no longer able to function or do the thing it was built to do. You can have a great-looking car but without the engine it is going nowhere.

The passengers will become disgruntled and have no choice but to get off and jump into another vehicle.

However, if the engine is working and especially if it is in immaculate condition, it will keep going even if the rest of the car is falling apart. You will always have some passengers and people wanting to join you on the journey.

The engine is probably the most important part of the vehicle and as long as it is intact your journey will continue.

Your cash flow is like the engine – if the cash in your company runs out then the business will cease to exist. As long as there is cash in the company your business will continue to survive and grow.

Fuel tank – Sources of income

If you ever run out of fuel then your journey will come to a temporary halt. As long as you are able to find the correct fuel your journey will continue.

Your journey should be planned in a manner so that you are aware of where the fuel stations are situated and when you are likely to need them to keep a constantly filled tank. There are many types of fuel: petrol, diesel and gas. If we fill our vehicle with the wrong fuel then that will damage our car. However if we modify our car to deal with *all* types of fuel then we can be on a great journey and find that fuel may never be an issue.

The different sources of income are like the fuel in your fuel tank because it keeps your business running.

The exhaust – The fixed expense

The exhaust represents the fixed expense in the company.

The exhaust releases the waste products from your vehicle. It represents the fixed expenses in your business. Every company has fixed costs and just like the exhaust fumes they cannot be avoided.

Steering wheel – Strategy direction

The steering wheel represents the strategy direction.

The driver controls the steering and can take the vehicle in any direction they want. The driver can turn corners, make U-turns and even change direction completely.

In any business it is important to know the big steps that you need to take in order to keep your business going in the right direction. If you steer your vehicle in the wrong way, you could easily lose your way.

Path ahead – Strategic action business plan

The path ahead represents the strategic action business plan and I call this the mighty action plan (MAP).

The path ahead is the route that you are taking to get to where you want to be. You can decide to take the fastest, the shortest, the toughest or any other alternative route that you want. However, if you have no specific destination, you may not like where you end up. The greater the clarity of where you want to go and where you want to be, the more clearly you can plan your journey. If you have a well-planned journey, you can be confident that the passengers and the driver are more likely to have a very successful and fulfilling ride.

If the driver is on the wrong path or driving in the wrong direction, the passengers will become angry, disappointed or even lose hope. If you have an idea of where you want to go, you can simply get in the car and drive. You may eventually get to your desired destination but without planning, it is a road that is likely to have many challenges and you can expect a much rougher ride.

On the other hand if the journey has been planned, including stops and refuelling, then you can expect a much smoother journey and you may even get to your destination faster.

When a driver knows that they are on the right path they can be confident of steering the vehicle smoothly and easily to where they want to go.

The MAP provides the detailed steps that must be taken in order to realise your business vision. As you make progress through the MAP it brings you closer to your destination, step by step.

Tyres – Staff

The tyres of the vehicle are the staff in your business. The tyres are very important to keep the vehicle moving. If the tyres are not looked after then the ride in the vehicle will become uncomfortable.

Sometimes one or more of the tyres may become a little flat in which case it will need pumping up; at other times you may have over filled it and may need to take out some of the air. If the treads on the tyres are worn out, driving the vehicle can become dangerous.

If the driver of the vehicle does not look after the tyres then the least he can expect is a rough ride and some unpleasant experiences. At worst the tyres can put the vehicle at risk and endanger the driver and the passengers in the car.

If the driver of the vehicle looks after the tyres and maintains them then the tyres will overcome all the bumps and cracks in the road and they can look forward to a safe and great journey ahead.

Your staff and your team need looking after. If you look after your team they will look after you and your business and help to keep your business safe.

Brakes – Challenges

The brakes in the vehicle represent the challenges in your business.

The brakes in any vehicle are used to slow it down or to stop it. If the road is clear and you are travelling to your destination, there is no need for the use of brakes.

The brakes are there as a safety mechanism to help slow the car down if it gets too fast and prevent it from getting out of control. They are also be needed to slow the car down when danger needs to be avoided.

If your brakes fail you are more than likely to lose control of the vehicle and inevitably be involved in an accident. In the worst case scenario the collision could be fatal, destroying the car in the process and, in this analogy, ending your business. Alternatively the car may just be damaged and the journey therefore stopped temporarily while repairs are taking place or if you are lucky, only superficial minor damages have occurred whereby the journey can continue without delay.

Look after and maintain your brakes and use them wisely to overcome dangerous situations and to ensure a safe and effective journey. It's worth remembering that overly cautious driving may also hinder the progress of your journey.

Responding inappropriately to the challenges in your business is like using your brakes inappropriately whilst driving. With care and consideration all the challenges can be handled in a suitable manner and you can continue your business.

Car body – Branding

The car body represents the branding of your business ... your promise.

There are many different types of car on the road. They appeal to people for different reasons. They make a different promise to the end user.

It may be the make or the design and shape or even the colour of the car. The state of the bodywork gives the onlooker the first impression of that vehicle.

Is the car clean and immaculate and does it attract people so that they want to join the driver on their journey?

Sometimes the vehicle looks pristine on the outside yet the interior is dirty, unkempt, ripped or damaged or alternatively there are cars that have a pristine interior with a damaged, rusty unkempt exterior. This lack of congruency may confuse your passengers and could affect the trust and relationship that exist between the occupants of the vehicle.

If the car body is beautiful and appealing and is matched by a neat and tidy interior then the driver can expect that lots of people will want to take a ride in their vehicle.

Your branding is like the car body because just like the body of the car you will be a magnet for those customers that share your values and promise.

Mirrors – Competition

The mirror represents the competition to your business.

The mirrors are often overlooked yet they represent an important part of the vehicle. You use the mirrors to keep an eye on what is happening around you. You will use them to park safely, pull out safely, change lanes carefully and even notice if any vehicles that are way behind you are catching up.

When a vehicle is being driven, the driver does not focus entirely on the mirrors otherwise they are unlikely to get very far. Hence, whilst it is important to keep an eye on them it is not essential to focus all of your energy on them.

Every safe driver will take a look in the mirror before deciding to manoeuvre their vehicle in a different direction or when changing lanes. To have a great journey the driver should focus on the road ahead, glancing in the mirror occasionally.

The competition is like the mirrors in the car because although it is important for us to keep an eye on our competition, they should not be the focus for our business.

Dashboard – Daily reports

The dashboard represents the daily figures that need to be observed.

Every vehicle has a dashboard and includes such things as the steering wheel, warning lights for engine malfunction, low fuel, low oil pressure etc. and displays for many other functions too.

It is imperative that you as the driver are keeping a regular eye on the dashboard. If there are any warning lights that come on then he needs to investigate it. If you choose to ignore it, then the damage to the vehicle could be fatal.

For example, if the oil or the engine malfunction light comes on, then these issues need to be dealt with immediately as this can directly impact the engine, sometimes damaging it permanently. The dashboard will not tell you what the problem is but will advise you that there is an issue that needs to be addressed. If the fuel gauge in your car is showing that it is becoming empty or low, then you as the driver knows that you need to fill up otherwise your vehicle is going to come to a halt soon. If the dashboard is not flashing any warning lights and all the measures are OK then you do not need to worry about the state of the vehicle and can focus completely on the road ahead.

The daily report is like having a dashboard because when there are things that stand out on any given day, you can take actions that will help the business grow or prevent it from losing profits.

Oil leaks – Avoidable wastage

An oil leak in the car represents the avoidable wastage of funds in your business.

If there is an oil leakage from your vehicle you should pay close attention to it. Running a vehicle that is drastically low on vital fluids can cause severe damage. Preventing or reducing the leaks in the engine will significantly improve the running of the vehicle.

The avoidable wastage of funds is like oil leaking from your car and by simply tightening a few bolts in your business you can avoid losing profit unnecessarily.

Indicators – Performance indicator

The indicators in a car represent the performance indicator of a business.

Indicators on a car are used to inform other road users of the driver's intent to turn or change lane towards that direction.

If the driver is indicating to turn in one direction and then decides to go in the other you can imagine what is likely to happen. There are three possible outcomes.

1. If there are no other road users on the road at the time, then the car will simply be heading in the wrong direction. If you as the driver decide to keep going down that same road then you are likely to be going a lot further away from where you want to go until you turn around and start heading back in the right direction.

2. If there are other road users, for example pedestrians or other vehicles, you could hurt others and also injure yourself and your passengers. This damage is repairable and you can get back on the road after the setback but you will be delayed on your journey; how much will be determined by the amount of damage that has occurred to all the vehicles, passengers and people involved. Eventually you will get back on the road.

3. If the driver is driving at speed on a busy motorway and indicates in one direction then changes lane in the opposite direction it could cause a very serious accident. It may cause serious injury to the driver and his passengers and could even be fatal.

When the driver is using his indicators correctly then he is being safe for himself, his passengers and other road users.

Performance indicators are like the indicators on a car because when you look at these parameters it will show you whether your business is heading in the right direction or not.

Gearbox – Marketing

The gearbox represents the marketing in your business.

I am sure that all of you who drive have at one time or another stalled your vehicle. This is when your vehicle stops suddenly because it is in the wrong gear.

For a smooth ride the driver needs to make sure that their vehicle is in the right gear at the right time. When the gearbox is used appropriately then acceleration can be achieved smoothly and effectively.

Your marketing needs to be appropriate and effective and should help you travel smoothly just like when your gears being used appropriately.

Speed – Growth

The speed of your vehicle represents the growth of your business.

Many people love speed. Fast is great ... well sometimes. Driving your vehicle too fast can hinder your ability to keep control of it. This can be dangerous for you and your passengers as well make the journey unpleasant. The chances of having an accident are increased and this can potentially derail your progress and cause considerable damage to your vehicle.

Driving very slowly can also be very painful and frustrating for the passengers and it is likely that you could end up losing them. Driving slowly will result in you reaching your destination later than you had anticipated and this could have its own repercussions.

A drive in your vehicle at a controlled speed, accelerating and decelerating gradually when needed, provides a much more enjoyable and pleasing journey. You are able to keep all of your passengers on board and possibly have more people wanting to join you.

The growth in your business can be measured just like speed in a car.

Servicing – Business review

Servicing your vehicle is like doing a business review.

Servicing is usually undertaken on a vehicle either when the vehicle has covered certain mileage, annually or when the dashboard indicates that a service is necessary.

There are two types of servicing. A basic service generally involves oil and oil filter change and new spark plugs or fuel filter. A more advanced and thorough service will include all the criteria from the basic service plus extras like lubricating of all working parts such as the hinges and catches and a safety check on the vehicle, for example on the tyres, steering, seat belt, wipers and so on.

A vehicle that is not serviced regularly compared to one that is regularly serviced is less fuel-efficient, less safe, less reliable and more likely to have a breakdown because faults may be overlooked until it is too late.

A vehicle that is serviced regularly will hold its value because it is being better maintained and naturally it will attract more buyers who are willing to pay higher prices.

A business review is like servicing your vehicle because it gives you an opportunity to evaluate your business and address anything that may need looking at, plan new strategies for the future and celebrate your business successes.

MOT – Annual P&L

The MOT (Ministry of Transport test) is like doing the annual P&L in a business.

The MOT is a thorough annual inspection of a vehicle to test for its safety, roadworthiness and exhaust emissions.

It is illegal to drive a vehicle on a public road without a current MOT certificate and is prerequisite for obtaining a tax disc. Some of the things that the MOT test covers are directional indicators, steering, brakes, tyres, body structure, exhaust and driver's view of the road, which includes the windscreen and mirrors.

Any car that has successfully passed its MOT test is able to be on the road for another year. It shows that the vehicle is in a healthy state and gives confidence to the passengers to continue their journey in the vehicle.

Similarly the annual P&L is like having an MOT. It shows you how well your business has performed in the last financial year and it assesses whether your business is fit to continue for the year ahead. Not forgetting that it will help you calculate your taxes and remind you that you need to pay them to keep your business open.

SUMMARY AND KEY LEARNING

The importance of having more than a business plan

A business plan alone is not enough with one in three businesses failing in their first year. You need a more robust framework to be successful in business.

Being passionate about anything will bring results.

Many of us are passionate about things in life but it is not always possible to make a living out of them.

There are many hidden resources that we have; we need to know how to take advantage of them.

Unity amongst all of the business partners is vital.

All business partners need to know the basics of business.

We need creativity and innovation in our business.

Understanding business is easy

Having your own business means that you must understand the basics. Often that can seem overwhelming and difficult.

Simply having a business plan is not enough and you need to be able to understand the basics so that you can use your passion and expertise to create a business that is successful.

The analogy of the vehicle will help you appreciate and understand the basics of business. This understanding will inspire you to appreciate the need for action and when to take it.

The vehicle analogy

It may seem a little farfetched at the moment – you may be wondering how this simple analogy can teach you to have a successful business. Well, by simply appreciating this analogy it will open your eyes to the issues and challenges in business. If you maintain your business in the same manner as a proud vehicle owner looks after his car then you too will have a successful business.

Everything does not need to be dealt with at the same time

Yes, there is a lot to know and do in running your own business but the great thing is that we do not need to do all of them at the same time. Just as we maintain our vehicle and tackle each issue at their appropriate time, we can do exactly the same in our business. However it is important to be aware of some things all of the time and we need to learn how to do that without becoming overwhelmed.

How do we overcome being overwhelmed?

We are all overwhelmed at times. So how can the vehicle help us deal with that?

The vehicle has been separated into three priorities. The first priority deals with you as the owner. This looks at your values, passion and vision and then addresses the viability of the business.

The second priority will assume that you have the required passion, vision and a viable business. Here we deal with the actions and steps needed to realise that vision. This priority will address all the steps that should be taken to move your business from concept to realisation.

The third priority will look at the tweaks in your business that will give you massive benefits and show when to take the steps that will improve your profits significantly. This priority will help you understand how you are progressing in your business, review your business and check in on progress towards your vision (are you still on the right path on your journey) and how you can maximise profit by tightening operations in your practice.

SO WHAT'S NEXT?

Understand the principles of business that have been shown to you through the vehicle analogy.

Go through the next chapter, which addresses the first priority and complete the exercise in that chapter. This will give you clarity and create a vision for your business.

You can download the framework and complete the exercise on your laptop. This will allow you to keep everything in one place on one page. Going through the chapters will give you the ability to realise exactly what is going on in your business at a glance.

IS IT TIME TO GET IN THE DRIVING SEAT?-THE FIRST PRIORITY.

There are only **TWO** things that a business owner needs to know about their business for it to be successful.

The first is do I have love and passion for my business? The second is will it make me any money?

For many people simply answering the first question is hard enough. There lots of people who get involved in business and they do not have any connection for the business that they are involved in and consequently they lose focus.

Let's imagine that one day you are approached by two budding entrepreneurs asking you to invest in their separate businesses. They both want to open a bookshop. Mark hates reading and cannot stand the sight of books. Sam is an avid reader and absolutely passionate about books; he can tell you about different covers, changes made to different editions; he even describes to you how the pages feel and smell and so on.

What do you think their results are going to be? Who do you think is likely to do well in their venture? Who do you think is going to deliver a better service to their customer? What are the likely outcomes of their businesses? If this was the only information you had to go on to make an investment and you had to invest, who would you go into partnership with?

I guess if you were forced to invest in one of these businesses, based on this information, it would be with Sam. This decision is based on the fact that Sam loves books, he has a passion for them and you may therefore expect him to be more committed. You would question Mark's motives for starting this business and possibly doubt his commitment too.

Now imagine the same situation but this time you know that Sam does not have a clue about business but Mark is a genuine businessman. This time making the investment would be harder to make. Your dilemma is that Sam is very passionate about what he wants to do but lacks business skills whereas Mark has good business skills and has the potential to make money but does he have the commitment to make things work? What will he do when and if things start to get difficult? Is he in it for the long haul?

Which of these two businesses would you invest in now?

This decision is not as easy to make. I guess that some of you would invest with Sam and others with Mark.

Now if you consider a situation in which both Mark and Sam have excellent business skills, who would you choose then? It becomes a no brainer: in this circumstance, I know that if I had to invest under these circumstances it would be in Sam every time.

The first priority of the 'your vehicle for business success' deals with both of these issues. In a simple three-step process it addresses your reasons, passions and values for your business and from this create an amazing and exciting business vision.

The second step is also a very simple three-step process that will determine whether you have a successful or can create a viable business.

The secret of establishing a successful business is that you are passionate about it and that it makes you money.

WHY DO I WANT TO DRIVE THIS VEHICLE/WHY DO I WANT TO BE IN BUSINESS/WHY AM I IN BUSINESS?

It is always important to know and understand your own reasons for being in business. Those people that do best at anything in life are those that love doing whatever it is that they are doing.

If your reasons for doing anything are powerful enough then you will find a way of doing those things. If you enjoy doing an activity then you are more likely to keep doing it more regularly. If you are passionate about a business or a product then you are more likely to succeed in that business than someone who is less enthusiastic about them.

Why do people go into business?

This is a very important question because if your reasons for going into business are not exciting or juicy enough then the relationship that you have with your business may become arduous.

Be your own boss

Many people go into business wanting to be their own boss because of their wish to be independent or be in control of their future. They want greater autonomy in their lives and this may be because they do not like being told what to do. Others may have had one or more bad or unfortunate experiences working for other people.

There are a few people who will give up their job to pursue a business career because they do not agree with the principles or the ethos of their employer.

A number of people will pursue owning their own business because there is a lack of opportunities for promotion or a rise in their salary from their present employer. Certain individuals who have just lost their job may feel that their only opportunity to earn a living is to start their own business.

Make more money

There is a belief amongst a lot of people that when you are working for yourself or running your own business you are making more money. This belief may come from knowing people who have become successful running their own business or perhaps from working in a business that appears to be very successful and making a good profit. A few business owners may buy flash cars and run up other unnecessary expenses when they start out to create an impression that they are successful – unfortunately many of them end up regretting their actions.

Make money from a great idea or a product

Some people will have a great idea or discover a product that they believe in and go on to pursue this as a business. Some ideas and products are outstanding and will make the owner a fortune; others have not been thought through so well and may lead to big losses and failure.

I remember as a 15-year-old, a sales rep came to my father's household and jewellery store to sell us imitation perfumes. I was absolutely sold on these perfumes and against my father's better judgement I persuaded him to buy loads of these. I mean you couldn't go wrong, these were copies of the biggest brands of the times Anais Anais, Chanel, Poison and many others. These big brands were being sold for £20 or £30 for a small bottle and here I had bottles of what I believed to be a very similar product that I was able to sell for a pound. It was an expensive mistake for me and an important lesson to learn because the two were very different and I was never able to sell them .

Gap in the market

Sometimes an opportunity in business will present itself and those with a vigilant eye will take advantage of this. There are times when an individual will be in the right place at the right time and realise that there is a demand for a service or a particular item. They will take advantage of this opportunity and situation and embark upon the venture.

Gets involved in or inherits the family business

This is as it says on the tin. This is an individual who simply slots into a role in a family business or organisation.

Enjoy business

Certain individuals are just born to do business. These are people who are very passionate about business and may have been motivated and inspired by something or someone in this field.

In truth lots of business owners end up working harder, for longer hours and earning a lot less money than being employed. Perhaps in this case their only real advantage is that they are their own boss but they probably give themselves a harder time than any employer ever did. In the end they become a slave to their business.

Can I just jump into it?

Many people just jump into a business without thinking about it. Even if it is a small corner shop, their thinking process may be: buy a bag of potatoes for £3.00, sell it for £5.00 and make a £2.00

profit. They almost forget that they need to take into account the rent, rates, taxes, salary for employees and many other factors. Although this is a little simplistic there are often many unforeseen surprises that crop up because the whole venture was either not planned at all or if planned it was done poorly.

When you are running your business, you may not have strategised effectively. On paper you are making a profit but in reality things might be very different. Imagine that you have just started a new business and to build up your customers and their loyalty, you decide to give your products out on credit. This credit is not backed up with any type of guarantee. Some of these customers have decided that they are not going to pay you or do not have the money to pay you. You are stuck. If you shut up shop, then you will never recover the money owed to you but on the other hand how long can you survive waiting for the money to arrive? Can you afford this loss? In the meantime how much loss are you prepared to incur?

A business plan is not enough

Most businesses will have a business plan of some sort. Some plans are very detailed, others simply exist in the business owner's head.

Some plans are created to raise money to fund their business, which is why it is written for that purpose only and ends up being only a paper exercise which is not thought through thoroughly enough. I remember many years ago a family friend showed me his business plan. He had a launderette and needed five new washing machines. At the time each machine cost £2000 each so he needed £10,000. He worked out from his experience that in the summer his business earned him £500 per month and in the winter £2000 per month. He considered eight months to be winter months and four months to be summer. The washing machine life expectancy was about 10 years. He took this note to an investor, who was convinced and the deal was done. This literally was his business plan. To his credit it worked out for him but that is not always the case with many businesses. These days investors are a lot more sceptical and need a lot more convincing for them to invest in other people's ventures.

Many business plans do not work because they are written, sometimes very quickly, to serve a purpose – for example to raise capital – after which it is stashed away in a drawer somewhere never to be found again.

Perhaps the business owner does not know what to put in business plan and so never truly attempts to write a comprehensive one. Hence the plan lacks the clarity and detail needed to make it work.

A lot of business owners never even write a business plan – their plan is simply in their heads (as mentioned earlier) because some of them are too busy working *in* their business rather than working *on* their business. This means that they sometimes miss big opportunities and cannot plan for sudden changes in the business environment. They often fail to see the bigger picture.

A lot of business owners fail to see how a business plan can benefit them. Once an entrepreneur has begun trading, their focus is for their business to survive; they become so involved in the day-to-day aspect of it that they cannot see how a plan is going to help them. Besides, writing a business plan can be very confusing and overwhelming and some business owners are unwilling to sacrifice their working and free time to do this.

Not the life that I had dreamt about?

Many business owners begin their enterprise and become so absorbed and involved that they do not have time to do anything else. I have met business owners that are very regretful because they let their business activities affect their relationship with their partner and children, their social life and their health.

Some business owners have a very successful business, a beautiful house and a great car. But imagine that one day they are affected by challenges to their health. Having damaged their relationship with their partner and children, they may now have the prospect of facing the future alone. It is at these moments they realise how the choices they have made have led to this point and that those people for whom this journey was started out are the very ones they have managed to distance and alienate. Stories like this are not uncommon.

Recently I met John. All he wanted was a successful business that provided for his family and a fulfilling life. He used to run a property portfolio and during the early days in his business, things seem to be ticking over well. He had made a lot of money and quickly.

In his low husky voice he told me that in the beginning when things were great, he used to spend all hours of his day finding property, negotiating deals and pleasing investors and clients. When the market turned he spent his time trying to pay the bills, finding prospects to buy the buildings that nobody now wanted and avoiding his previous clients and investors. It almost cost him his marriage and children, it adversely affected his health, he lost five years in that business and was now heavily in debt. This certainly was not the life that he had dreamt of when starting his enterprise.

Why are my values important in running my business?

Values are a set of internal filters that determine an individual's model of the world. A value is simply what is important to a person in terms of their career, relationship, business and so on. Here we will focus on what is important and has value for an individual as a business owner.

This is important because it will create momentum in the business when the values are aligned. It will give clarity when creating a business vision. It will strengthen the company vision, purpose, mission and action plan when the values are shared in the company. It creates an effective means of understanding and managing teams when individual value system are recognised and utilised.

Why should my business have a vision?

When you have a vision for your business, it is like having an adrenaline rush every day. Before that vision has been realised you can see it, feel it, hear the sounds that come from it, smell the cake as you are baking it and almost taste the sweet taste of success.

A vision is a very powerful tool and the greater the clarity you have, the greater the momentum and the greater the chances of success.

Ten years after buying my business the local health authority, then known as a Primary Care Trust (PCT), were running the surgery across the road from my pharmacy and this generated about 60 per cent of pharmacy income at the time. They had planned to close it and move all of the patients to a new purpose-built surgery about a mile from there. I could see that this would have huge implications for my business and the plans that I had to serve the community would go out of the window.

We had just moved back into our purpose-built premises, having invested almost half a million pounds in the project. We had created the country's first pharmacy and wellbeing centre. The vision was to create a pharmacy with consulting and treatment rooms that would facilitate consultations with pharmacists, doctors, nurses and other professionals, screening services, alternative therapies such as remedial sports massage, reflexology and others and then have a conference room that would allow training and education programmes for patients, the wider community and health professionals. Some of the services would be private (i.e. patients would pay), some would be delivered for free to support the community and educational events would be delivered by a team of multidisciplinary volunteers. Some elements of this vision were already being delivered from our facilities.

I went to the PCT and shared my vision with them. Luckily for me they decided to keep the surgery running and chose to invest £1m, buying the premises next to it and merging the two buildings so that the practice became fit for purpose. My business has grown by 80 per cent since I rebuilt my facilities.

Success in business

The more love and passion you have for something, the more you are going to enjoy doing it. The more you enjoy doing something, the more you will do it and the better you will get at it. If you have a business idea or product that you are passionate about then there is a greater likelihood that you are on the path to success.

However, just being passionate is not enough for success. There needs to be a demand in the market for that product or service. Therefore, market research should be undertaken. Furthermore, a realistic cash flow projection should be carried out so that you can determine whether the business proposition has a genuine chance to succeed.

The first priority of 'your vehicle for business success' will deal with both of these issues using a simple three-step process. The first step will address your reasons, passions and values for your business and from this you move onto the second step to create your amazing and exciting business vision.

The third step will determine whether you have a successful or can create a viable business.

WHAT YOU NEED TO KNOW BEFORE YOU JUMP INTO THE DRIVING SEAT

The Driver – Business owner

Often new business owners underestimate what is involved in running their own business. Hence they fail to plan for it, can be overwhelmed and thus lose interest.

The business owner (or driver) must have clarity and purpose for going into business. They must ask the question, 'What do I want to achieve in my life?' This is as important as any-thing else in business. If you are aware of what type of life you want you can start to prepare for it. Have the bigger picture in front of you, always. When the going gets tough this could be the motivation that sees you succeed where others have failed.

What do I know about my business and what do I need to know?

This is something that many people never ask themselves. They have a great idea and they think that they know it all. The biggest mistake that many business owners make is that they start believing that everyone holds the same belief about their business or product that they do. If you have love and passion for what it is that you want to do then any research that is undertaken will feel like a hobby and not like pain.

What is important to me in my business?

This is simply what a business owner values in their business.

These values can come from family, friends, religion, school, geography and demographics, economics, media and significant emotional events (this list is not exhaustive).

Example of values

Authenticity	Faith	Honesty	Respect
Charisma	Freedom	Leadership	Strength
Communication	Fulfilling	Love	Responsibility
Creativity	Fun	Passion	Team
Efficiency	Health	Peace	Truth
Excellence	Helping people	Perseverance	Wealth

When most or all of your values are met it means that you are getting and doing whatever it is that is important to you. As a result it will create a greater motivation towards your goals.

What do I want to create in my business and how does that support the life that I want?

This is extremely valuable to know because this becomes the reference for where you will be taking your business. This is what you want to be telling yourself over and over again because it will create the momentum that will take you there. If someone knocks on your door and drops off cement, bricks and other building materials it is hard to get excited about it unless you have decided that you want to build an extension.

Remember you will be looking at more than just what you want to create in your business it is looking at your life too. Once you have answered this question then you know what type of commitment and effort will be needed to deliver this.

How do I feel about my business so far?

Having worked out your reasons, motivation and inspiration for the business, it is time to evaluate how you feel about the whole thing. If you are not overly enthused by the enterprise then it is important to address this and consider changing the focus of your venture.

If it feels absolutely the right thing to do and you are excited and driven by the future prospect then it is time to look at what to do about it.

Will it make me any money?

Now that you feel the passion for your business then it is time to consider whether it will make you any money.

This is a very easy three-step process.

1. What are the sources of income in the business? This is just to see all the possible angles from which this business can generate an income.

2. What are the costs, especially the fixed costs? We need to look at this realistically and be honest with ourselves.

3. Cash flow. If your cash flow is finished then your business is over. Having looked at our income and our expenditure, you need to see how much money you will need to begin your enterprise, where else you can

generate cash if you need to and how long will it last us if things do not work out as planned.

These steps are extremely important because they can show you how long you can expect to stay in business if you make no profit at all, whether it be three months, six months, a year or longer. When your business makes profit you extend its life. When your enterprise begins to make sales, whether it is goods or services that you sell, and profit, some business owners start to spend lavishly and begin to take the money out of the company unnecessarily. This is not necessarily wrong if your cash flow is healthy but it could be detrimental if it has a huge impact on your cash flow.

If the driver likes his car, gets in and finds that the interior is perfect, the windscreen is clear, the engine is running smoothly, the fuel tank is full and the exhaust is there but emitting nothing to worry about then they know that they are going on a great journey. The drive is going to be fun, enjoyable and fulfilling.

IS THIS THE VEHICLE FOR MY BUSINESS SUCCESS?

It is all well and good talking about the model theoretically but how can it be put into action? The answer to that question is easy, simply complete the exercises below.

This section involves doing some home play... if you want to maximise the benefits to your business then it will involve making notes. To help you it may be useful to visit our website, www. yourvehicleforbusinesssuccess.com to look at the case studies that relate to each section and perhaps even download the template to keep all your information in one place.

Driver's motives – Your (the business owner) motives.
Exercise 1

Answer each one of these questions

- Why do I want to go into this business?

- What do I want to achieve in my life?

- What do I know about my business and what do I need to know?

- How does your business support the life that you want?

- What is important to you in your business?

Having answered these questions there will be some clarity about your aims and goals that you want from your business. It will also help you address your reasons for going into business.

The car interior/your business values

This exercise is extremely important. This deals with everything that is important to you in running your business.

For this exercise part 1, part 2 and pat 3, it will be useful to ask a business partner or a friend to take you through it.

Exercise 2

Part 1 – Discovering your values

Values will be either single words or short phrases.

Ask your friend or business partner to read the line below and you simply need to tell him/her all the words that come into your mind. Ask them to write them down for you. During this exercise you want spontaneous answers, not ones that you come up with after thinking about it for 30 seconds or so. You list everything until you come to a halt, this is called coming to a blank spot, repeat this twice more, asking your partner to continue recording on the same sheet. To achieve your complete list of values you will need to go through two blank spots.

'What is important to you in the context of your business?'

Part 2 – Discovering your motivation

This part of the exercise will help you discover your motivation strategy. To carry out this exercise you will need to recall three different and specific incidents when you were very motivated and inspired in the proposed business or any other business activity that you may have been involved with.

Ask your friend or partner to read the script below and record your answers.

> 'Now I want you to just stop, and remember a specific incident when you were totally motivated in the context of your business? As you go back to that time now, step into your body, see what you saw at the time, hear what you heard and feel the feelings of being totally motivated.

Now rewind the movie just a bit and tell me, what was the name of the feeling or emotion that was present just prior to the feeling of being totally motivated?'

For each value given in part 2 of the exercise, ask:

'So is_____ important to you in the context of your business?'

If yes, add to values list in part 1 of this exercise. If no go on until all values identified in part 2 of the exercise have been covered then elicit other values from a separate incident by repeating part 2 of the exercise two more times using two different incidents.

Once you have completed this exercise three times go onto part 3.

Part 3

This is to establish your threshold values.

Ask your friend or partner to read the script below and record your answers

Showing the whole list completed in part 1 and part 2, ask:

'OK, now take a look at this list, and all these values being present is there anything that would have to happen such that it would cause you to leave? Or stop?'

Wait for response. If a threshold value is given then ask putting their threshold value in the blank:

'So is _____important to you in the context of your business?'

Remember; if the threshold value is stated in the negative do not convert it to the positive. Add it to their value list as it was stated.

After that say:

> 'Now if all of these values were present and whatever they had stated as their threshold value occurred, is there anything else that would have to happen that would cause you to stay (or continue)?'

Add this to your value list. Repeat part 3, three times.

The combined list of values from part 1, 2 and 3 is the list of your values. This represents values, emotions and feelings that are important to you in the context of your business. The significant because it will help you stay motivated and committed to your business. When these values are met within your business it means that you are fulfilled and content because everything that is of consequence to you is being achieved.

Windscreen – Clear vision

Creating a vision for your business is very important. This vision should take into consideration your motives that you have discovered in exercise 1 and your values that you have elicited in exercise 2.

Exercise 3

Using your answers from the driver's exercise and the values exercise create the vision for your business.

You can draw a picture or a diagram to represent your vision.

Once you have created your vision answer the questions below.

Do I have passion for what I am about to create in my business?

Now that you have created your vision, how do you feel about it?

Can you feel the fire in your stomach? Do you have passion for your business?

If the answers to these questions are either very positive or a definite yes, then you know that you have a business for which you have passion and now you can look forward to seeing if it is a viable one.

Fuel tank – What are the sources of my income?

You now have a business for which you have love and passion so now you need to address how you are going to make it work for you.

Imagine a mighty river that is flowing and from it flow many little streams. Each stream waters and feeds the land surrounding it.

This is your income stream.

Exercise 4

To determine your business income stream complete the questions below.

List all the things that will become part of your income stream for your business.

List separately all of the different retail section in your business, all the different service sectors within your business and anything that can be sold from your business that is allied to your business (linked sales).

These lists are the sources of income for your business.

Exhaust – Fixed expenses

Now you know the income stream. You now need to address the exhaust.

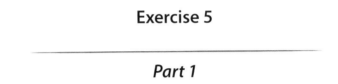

Exercise 5

Part 1

What are the fixed costs in your business?

This should include things like rent, rates, utilities, mortgage cost, salary, cost of delivery, stationery and so on.

Also include any fees or costs that you pay once a year, break it down to a monthly figure. You may want to add expenses that you incur occasionally for example your marketing cost which can be then worked out as cost per month.

List the fixed costs that occur in your business on a monthly basis in a table like the one below.

Part 2

List the expenses in your business that are considered one off costs, this may include things like fixtures and fittings, legal fees when setting up or any equipment that you may have bought.

The fixed costs are an indication of your monthly cost for running your business, part 1 of this exercise.

Your variable costs are the occasional expenses that are incurred by your business, for example marketing costs or cost of repairs, we have accounted for this in the fixed cost aspect of the calculation also in part 1 of this exercise.

This is the list and cost of your fixed expenses in your business every month or every year. When your business can cover these expenses it is breaking even, provided that there are no other costs that you have forgotten to take into consideration.

Your one off cost is the set up cost for your business, part 2 of this exercise. This is the initial investment that you will need to make to get your business up and running. To survive in business you will need to have funds available to pay for the monthly costs, the amount you calculated in part 1 of this exercise. This fund will comprise of the capital introduced into the company and the money raised from sales.

The Engine – Cash flow

The cash flow is the power behind your business. This needs to be positive all the while for your business to survive.

Exercise 6

For this exercise you will need to consider how much money you are willing to invest to begin your enterprise. We will look at this as cash introduced.

With this amount in mind, carry out the following exercise.

Part 1

Cash introduced

One off expenses

Cost per month

Cash balance

The balance here is the amount of money that you have left over after your set up cost and you have traded for a month. This exercise assumes that you have made no sales in the first month of trading.

Part 2

Cash balance (A)	
Fixed expenses per month (B)	
Life expectancy of your business without sales A/B	

If you divide the cash balance by the fixed expenses per month, you will work out how long your business will survive if you were to make no sales.

Although this is not an exact or an accurate measure of how long your business will survive, it is a good guideline to help you consider if your business is worth investing in or how much money you may need to invest to make it work.

You should carry out a cash flow balance calculation every month in business. Cash flow balance calculation is simply calculating how much money you have in hand and in the bank and subtracting your monthly expenses, this will leave you with the amount of money (cash) that you will have left after all of your expenses have been paid. If you notice that your cash flow is running low, you would then have enough time to find funds to reinvest in your venture.

Can I see profit in my business?

To project a more realistic cash flow calculation you can add the estimated income from your income streams to the cash balance for each month. If from your projections and cash flow calculations for three years there is a positive cash balance then the chances of success and survival in your business venture is very good. This is because most businesses fail within the first three years.

If your cash flow is positive and increasing without you having to introduce any more money into the business then it means that your enterprise is making a profit.

SHOULD I START THE ENGINE?

Working through this chapter you will have learned:

What is motivating you to start your own business and in doing so, whether you have love and passion for it.

The significance of your business values and how to elicit them.

The importance of having a vision for your business and how you can create one using your motivation for going into your venture and your business values.

What your income streams are.

What your set up cost for your business is.

What the minimum running costs for your business per month are.

The life expectancy of your business from what you are willing to invest and if you make no sales.

How much you need to invest to make your business viable.

You can now answer the two questions that a business owner needs to know about their business for it to be successful.

The first question is do I love and have passion for my business? The second question is will it make me any money?

If the answer to both of these questions is yes then you are now ready to get in the driving seat to start the engine and take your business vehicle for a drive.

LET'S TAKE THE VEHICLE FOR A SPIN—THE SECOND PRIORITY

DO YOU WANT A SMOOTH RIDE?

By the time you reach this stage, you should know that you are passionate about the business that you are involved in or about to begin, you have created an amazing vision for your business that meets all of your values and it is a financially sustainable and profitable venture for you. In other words you have started the engine of your car and it is now ready to be taken for a spin.

I am sure you often get great ideas but how many times have you done anything about it? So far you have carried out your due diligence and are able to appreciate that there is a business that you can now establish. Just this realisation can create for you a state of being overwhelmed, excitement and then fear. At this point all of your self-confidence is tested and doubts starts to creep in. Often the very people you trust and those that are genuinely concerned for you scare you with stories of the prospect of failure and how that will cost you. At a time when you need your loved ones and friends to support you and believe in you their words of caution cause you to procrastinate or worse still stop you from taking any action at all.

Running your business can be easy and be very fulfilling. You can have whatever it is that you desire but you need to take appropriate action to achieve your goals.

This chapter will look at how you can take your dream business and make it into a reality. This might seem like a fairytale, but this is one story that you can create and deliver.

In six very easy and simple steps you will be able to identify your resources, plan your business structure, commit to your brand, learn how to recruit appropriate staff and how to deal with your competition.

To do this you need to be resourceful, driven, inspired, determined and committed. It really is a time to get excited and time to take action. What you need at this stage is composure and direction, the opportunity to take a deep breath and strategise. This chapter will help you to discover the resources that will support your vision and assist you to deliver it. It will remove the feeling of being overwhelmed by facilitating the planning of the big and detailed steps for your business.

In this chapter and whilst working through the second priority will guide you to find the ideal employee, tell you what to look for and when and it will show you how to create an outstanding team that will grow with your business.

You will also address the importance of branding and establish the promise that you make to your customers. In this section you will find innovative strategies to tackle the difficulties and problems that could arise in your business and finally you will learn how to look at and deal with the competition in your business.

Passengers or hostages

In your business you will establish relationships; these are the passengers in your car. If you decide to take some people for a ride and they come willingly then they have come to enjoy the drive. If they have been forced into the vehicle then they will be looking for opportunities to escape – they are then your hostages. Some people will begin the journey happily but then something may happen that will make them want to get out and leave. The relationships that you have with your business partners, customers and network need to be well maintained and nurtured otherwise it will pose difficult challenges moving forward.

As a business owner it is essential to understand your own strengths and weaknesses with respect to your business. This will help you focus on those areas and you can either outsource, get help or skill yourself up to address areas of weakness. If you are in a partnership you can support each other by taking on roles in your strong positions and get others to work in areas that they are good at. This way all of your weak areas can be dealt with. This is a good time to take a look at yourself because it will help you pinpoint your strengths and when you focus on them you will make faster progress. This will give you and your business momentum and motivation to keep going. If you were able to bring in the right person, through your partners or network, to concentrate and work in areas where you need help it would make your business run more efficiently.

Business Partners
I have heard many people mention that they could not have partners in their business. Potential issues can lead to long-term family problems, longstanding friendships becoming destroyed and feuds that can last for years.

How many of you have met people that have been in business with others and have heard about their bad experience? This happens because there is a lack of communication, differences in values and expectations and sometimes not knowing the people that you go into partnership with well enough. There are plenty of other reasons too. Does that mean that partnerships should be avoided at all cost, even if new relationships have the potential to take your business to a whole new level of success and profitability?

Remember that Rome was not built in a day and nor did the empire become so vast by the actions of one person. It needed a huge army and thousands of people working in a team and having a relationship that supported the grand vision. Similarly business partnership that are harnessed and supported will help establish and build an amazing business.

A great business partnership will bring enormous benefits. The advantage of having many people in the partnership can mean greater commitment to your vision and each one will bring their own skill mix and set of experience that will benefit the team.

Business relationships break down because things are not made very clear from the outset. Humans are meaning making machines, we create all sorts of meanings from our experiences, sometimes their expectations are very different from their partners and when expectations are not met it leads to a lack of trust and resentment. Sometimes expectations from one or more of the partners are unrealistic and unreasonable. You can avoid this happening by having an open dialogue and having clarity for your business and then understanding the values and needs of everyone in the partnership. Fulfilling whatever is important to the individuals in the team will mean that there is fulfilment and trust in the team. The understanding of your own strength and weaknesses will help you identify your own needs and where you can support others. Being able to identify your partners' strengths and weaknesses means you can ask for help where you are weak and offer support in areas where you are strong. This will create unity in the team and a positive momentum towards your goal.

Customers

Perhaps the most important passenger is the customer. Ultimately it is the customer who is going to give fuel to the car to keep it going. It is important to find customers for your business and if you endeavour to deliver an outstanding product, one that will serve the needs of those that buy into your service, you are doing yourself and your community an injustice if you fail to sell your goods to help more people. You are not after the hard sell but rather an effortless selling and in the process hoping to create raving fans that will support and bring more business to your company.

Often it is easier to sell more to existing customers than find new ones. Consider two rivers, both of them 10 miles from you. The first river is called scarce. In this river there are very few fish whereas in the other river, which is called abundance, there are many. If you had to go fishing which of the two rivers would you go to?

Knowing and understanding your ideal customer is like fishing in the river of abundance. This will help you identify their challenges, needs and what keeps them awake at night, where you can find them and what their solution is. If you can deliver a solution to their problem then they will most likely do business with you. It will also ensure that you work intelligently and effectively so that you are not wasting time targeting business that does not need you. This will help you save money by marketing to your target customer and this clever marketing strategy will ensure that you reap a lot more reward than can be expected if your advertising is across the board to everybody and anybody. Once you can help your ideal customer they can become your advocates in the community, drumming up more business for you. If you managed to profile customer before you started your business venture then it will also give you an insight into the type of people you will be serving and this may allow you to consider or decide whether these are people that you want to be in business with.

Your network

Your network is a very powerful resource. People in your network can be the ones that you can go to for practical assistance, support and guidance when the going gets tough. Your network is full of people that share goodwill for you and your business venture. Often we do not have the courage to ask the people that we know for help and guidance because we do not want to be in a position of being rejected. Can we do something that will ensure that the chances of rejection are limited? The answer to that question is yes. If we understand the needs of the people in our circle and give them help and support when they need it without prejudice or expectations then that act of kindness will have a small or even a significant impact on them. It will strengthen your relationship with them.

A good example of how a strong network can benefit you is illustrated by an experience I had some years ago. On January 1, 2005, the Royal Pharmaceutical Society of GB introduced a requirement for pharmacists to put in place and operate written Standard Operating Procedures (SOPs) within individual pharmacies covering the dispensing process. This was initiated to comply with clinical governance requirements, healthcare professions were being required to put in place strategies for risk management and harm minimisation. For many pharmacies this was a huge challenge because it was a way of working differently and they were not used to having this as part of their practice. Many of us were overwhelmed with the thought of writing them. A friend and a pharmacist, who used to work as a manager for a large chain of pharmacies, came to see me and offered to give me copies of the SOPs that were written by his company so that I could use them to help me write the SOPs for my business. He did this without me asking him and I never forgot that act of kindness. A few years after that event he came to see me one day and offered to help me set up the wholesale division of my business. I accepted his proposal and we went into business together because I already had a lot of respect and trust for him. That area of our business has grown and we have been very successful with it, the rest is history.

Holding the steering wheel

When you are in a car, the person who is holding the steering wheel is in control of the vehicle and can take the car in whatever direction they choose. Similarly in your business you are the one in control and you have to steer your business in the right direction. You have created a vision for your business and now you need to take action to achieve that vision.

To give your business vision the best possible chance of success and to make the process manageable and effective it is important to identify all the tasks that need to be completed in the process of achieving your objectives. This process helps you stay focused on what is important and as you pass each milestone you know that you are making progress. This is like driving from home to a destination and on the route passing well-known landmarks.

If there are several partners in the business then the big steps can be divided amongst the team and each partner can take the responsibility for a task. Knowing the big steps means that we can then prioritise them in accordance with their importance and can focus on the things in the business that will give us the best results.

Focus on the path ahead

This follows on from taking control of the steering wheel. The path ahead deals with getting over all the hurdles, the turns that you need to take, when to take on your passengers, when to change or invest in new tyres (or staff) – in other words it is all appropriate actions that need to happen in order for you to reach you business targets. These are the gritty, detail steps that need to be taken to get the results that you want. We can consider steering the vehicle to be the theoretical part of the plan and the path ahead to be the practical plan for the business.

If there are partners in your business than all of the objectives can be divided between the partners, each one concentrating on an area of their strength. This would mean that the team is not overwhelmed and allows them to focus on the plan in hand.

This step should be carried out with as much detail as possible and should also include the member of the team responsible for each task. This will give clarity to what needs to be done and ensure that whoever in the team has been given a responsibility is accountable to the other members in the team and themselves to complete their undertaking. This process will help create clarity in your vision and it will also be an inspiration for the team when they are making progress.

When you are planning, sometimes you can highlight more efficient ways of doing things; it will keep you focused on achieving your mission and you can utilise your network to support you in establishing your business.

It is quite common to overestimate what you can do in a day but greatly underestimate what you can achieve in a year.

Car Body – Branding

Your brand is simply your promise to your customers. It tells them what they can expect from your products and services and it distinguishes you from your competitors. Your branding is who you are, who you want to be and who people perceive you to be. Every single business is a brand, whether it is a strong brand or a weak one. Each one of them makes a promise to their customers.

A brand is the heart and mind space given to your business by your customer. What images and feelings do you get when you see the logos and hear the names of the following companies: Coke, McDonalds, Disney, Nike? This perception is very important because if it does not inspire a favourable image or value for you in your heart and mind spaces then you are less likely to use or buy their products and services. If on the other hand you have favourable feelings towards these brands then they no longer need to convince you to buy their product because you already have an affinity for them.

Hence, the advantage of having a great brand is that it creates trust and confidence in your products and services. This will inevitably increase your sales and profit. It also helps your customers to differentiate you from other companies and businesses that are providing the same or similar services to yours.

Do I have good tyres?

Every vehicle should have tyres that are roadworthy otherwise it could lead to accidents, which can sometimes be fatal. Every business, if it continues to grow, will at some time need to employ people. These should be the business's most prized assets and therefore it is vital that you employ those that have the correct skill mix, attitudes and ambitions that meet the needs of the business. This is the team that will fulfil your ambitions and goals. When you employ someone who is appropriate for the business, they will strive for you, they will represent you and they will celebrate with you when reach milestones and complete your goals.

It is essential that you find outstanding individual/s to fit into your team and that you retain their services so that they help you grow while you help them grow too. A great employee can attract many customers and a poor one can lose them. Imagine that you employed an amazing young man as part of your sales team. His ability to connect with your customers and team means that he delivers a great service, which will often result in retaining the customer for more business in the future and will make them likely to recommend your business to their friends and colleagues.

Conversely, if your salesperson gave a terrible service then it is unlikely that the customer will come back and it is very likely that they will tell their friends and colleagues about the poor service that they received. If this experience became the norm then you could expect customers to start losing confidence in your business very quickly.

Having a good team also builds a great workplace environment and this in turn will motivate your workers to come in to work with a positive attitude. They will not consider coming to work a burden and this will result in better performance. The greater the trust and confidence between the employer and the employee, the greater the team. This positive energy is then transferred onto the shop floor and to the customers, resulting in greater confidence, trust and sales in your business and for your brand.

Once you find great employees, you must retain them. This will help the growth of your business and maintain the continuity of service. Everybody likes to be valued and if you value your employees, they will reciprocate. Therefore, if you find out what is important to them –it is not always money – and you provide that for them then it is very unlikely that they will leave.

Having a great team will accelerate your business growth and will create a positive and fantastic atmosphere to work in.

Why are the brakes in my car sticking while I am driving?

Although we may anticipate that there will be challenges in our business, often we do not give them much thought and usually things happen when we least expect them to. Sometimes the solution is simple and we can deal with it very easily while at other times it can be a very delicate and difficult situation that may bring the whole business to a standstill.

However much we prepare for the challenges in our business, we can never prepare for everything. Yet, if we are prepared for some of the eventualities that could happen then we really save ourselves a lot of time, money and stress. Many business owners are so engrossed into the day to day running of the business they just react to challenges as they arise. This fire-fighting approach can become tiresome and stressful and causes the business owner to lose focus.

Imagine that you are the owner of a frozen food store and during the night there is a power cut. What are the likely implications? If there is no alarm set up then you may not be aware that the power cut has occurred and if the outage lasts a while you may lose a lot of stock. You may need to close the shop down to clear up, there may be loss of earnings and you would undoubtedly become very stressed. If you have a strategy to deal with this sort of emergency then you simply apply the process and deal with the matter. Had you invested in freezers that have an emergency 12-hour backup power supply, you could expect that your food supply would be safe for at least another 12 hours if you ever had a power cut. This gives you the opportunity to find another source of power or find a friend with the necessary facilities to store your stock until things are back to normal.

With this process you can identify as many problems that you can think of, actions that you can take and who can help you in the process and how. This will allow you to deal with many of the issues efficiently and effectively, saving you time, money and stress.

Keep an eye on the mirror

When you are driving you keep an eye on the mirror so that you know that you are safe, that other vehicles are not too close to you and that you are OK to change direction. Whilst driving, you do not focus just on the mirrors; you are actually looking ahead and using the mirrors as a guide.

Similarly it is important to keep an eye on your competition but not to make it the focus for your business. Competition in business is actually very good because it improves the quality of service to the customer, it gives them better value for money and it gives them more choice. If your competitor opens near you or you open your business near your competitor, don't worry – it will actually draw more customers and people towards your business.

A few years ago there were only a couple of shops that sold clothes in a street, in Spinney Hill in Leicester, with many shops. Within five years four other shops had opened to sell clothes. You would anticipate that the first shop owner was now making less of a profit. In truth he made a lot more money because now the area had become renowned for the clothes shops and so when people in the city needed clothes for any occasion they would flock to the area because they knew that they would get exceptional prices, lots of choice and great customer service. As a result it was a win-win situation for all as long as they kept their standards high. Some of the shops did close and others opened in their place and those that closed were the ones that focused solely on their competition and competed on price alone. Those that were successful were the ones that focused on their brand, had a strategy to be different that met the needs of their customers and then stuck to their vision.

Competition is not a threat but an opportunity to grow your business. It is important to create your brand and know and understand your market so that you are current and have an appreciation for what your competition is doing so that you can make the necessary changes in your business should the need occur.

THE KEY TO YOUR CAR

What must you know before you go for a spin?

Once you have a passionate vision and a financially viable business then there are several things that need to happen for that venture to be realised.

It is important to understand yourself before you jump into a business. What are your strengths and what are your weaknesses? This will help you decide how you can move your business forward in a manner that serves you. You can focus in areas that you are strong and get help or learn the skills to address those areas in which you are weak. It is very important that you understand and address the help that you need to make your business a success.

It is important to understand the strengths and weaknesses of your business partner/s, and any other business that you partner or do business with, so that you can maximise the benefit of that relationship. This will help you understand yourself and your business partners and see how you can work efficiently and harmoniously. If you know what help you want, you can be specific in your request. This process will help you get that support.

The network table is your database of well wishers, friends and associates or people that you have come across that may be of help to you in your business, this is your magic resource pot. It will list the people or businesses that you know who can benefit and support you. Sometimes it is not apparent how some of these people can help but simply listing their areas of strengths may be of use to you should the need ever arise. The network table is also a relationship building exercise because life is not always just about you, helping others will always pay dividends in one way or another, either directly or indirectly. By simply acknowledging and then either providing or guiding someone through their difficult situation will establish a huge amount of goodwill that can be utilised in the future if needed.

This model will help you understand the mindset and the problem in detail for your ideal customer. This will help you understand the background, lifestyle and challenges of your ideal customer. Knowing this allows you to focus on providing the best solution for their needs, which then allows you to go out and find them. This process will help you identify your ideal customer and their challenges and it will help you discover where you can find them.

What action do I have to take?

Now you are in the following situation. You have or are deciding to go into a business for which you have a passion and love. You know that it is a financially viable business and have created a vision for the future of that business. You have made a conscious decision to think about your strengths and weaknesses and looked at what help you need to make this business a success. If you are going to work in a partnership, you have highlighted everyone's strengths and weaknesses and established the best working relationships. All of this and still there is no action. So now it is time to focus. You must identify what needs to happen to realise the vision for your business. This is all the things that have to happen in order to take your business to where you want it to be. This process will help you overcome being overwhelmed by making the whole establishing process easy, breaking it down into a number of manageable steps.

Staying on the right path

Now that you have come this far, it is essential that you stay focused and keep moving in the right direction. Now that you have identified all the steps that will ensure that your business gets to where it needs to, those steps need to be taken.

This is the stage where you need to go into details of what needs to happen to complete each step, when it needs to happen by and who needs to do what tasks.

During this task you can identify which member of your team, partnership or network can support you to reach your goals. As each task is being completed you are getting closer to where you want to be. In this process you can decide when you want to employ other people, what areas of your business you want to focus on first and then how you intend to grow your business.

This is perhaps one of the most important parts of the vehicle. If you plan this out correctly, this will become the blueprint for your business. This becomes your strategic business action plan and should help you to reach your goal.

What makes good tyres?

How do you know that you have got good employees or that you are employing the right person for the job? It is no good if you employ a chartered accountant to work in your business as a shop floor assistant or a cashier. If you are paying them the rate of a cashier they will feel undervalued, disinterested because this is not what they have trained to do and their performance may be substandard because they are not motivated or inspired in their employment. If you were paying them the rate of a chartered accountant the points above will still hold true because you are not using them in their area of strength. It is like getting a centre forward to play as a left back defender in football.

Here you need to determine what is the job description of the person you want to employ, what qualities do you want them to have and what values? Once you have clarity on these issues, you need to find someone who meets all of these criteria and then you will find your ideal candidate for the post. Obviously you still need to complete due diligence on the candidate and ensure that they actually do have all the qualifications that have been specified on their CV or application form, their references are genuine and appropriate and that they are delivering during their first few months of probation.

What is my promise?

Branding is the process involved in creating a unique name and image for your business in the heart and mind of your customers through presenting a consistent theme. This can exist in five different ways as explained by Daniel Wagner in his book, *Expert Success*. In your business these are present as brand absence where customers do not care where they buy from. Brand awareness is when customers notice that there is a brand connected to the business, it is not strong enough to drive business your way all of the time but can influence the decision to trade with you sometimes. Brand preference is where your customer will choose to do business with you over other similar businesses and they will associate with your company and will have a sense of belonging. However, if you are closed or cannot deliver a service within a certain time, this customer will shop elsewhere. Brand insistence is the stage when your customer will only do business with you. If they cannot find what it is that they want they will not take their business elsewhere. Brand advocacy is where your customers will have such a sense of belonging that they will spend their time and money to influence others to do business with you.

So the perception that people have of your business is going to place them in any of these five categories. When you have customers that prefer your brand over others, insist on your brand and become advocates of your business then price no longer is an issue as they are your loyal customers. You can simply stumble into creating your brand or consciously decide to build a brand from the outset. You cannot be all things to all people but you can be all things to some people and these are your ideal customers. You can build your brand based on your values, your vision and your ideal customer.

What makes my brakes stick? The challenges in my business

Every business will have challenges and problems from time to time. Some of them are predictable and others we have no control over and are totally unpredictable. Despite being able to foresee some of the issues that can affect our business many of us are never prepared to deal with them and are in a reactive mode when things go pear shaped. In the fire-fighting situation we sometimes do not make the most appropriate decisions because there can be a lot of pressure and we do not or may not have the time to think things through properly. If you imagine that your computer is being corrupted by a virus, all the data and hard drive would be destroyed or lost if the was no anti-virus protecting it. This is what I call the bug buster, it protects your business from being bugged or corrupted by unexpected problems or issues. The challenges to your brakes can become the go to section whenever your business has an issue that need resolving.

What do I look for in my mirror?

In every sphere of business there is competition. It is competition that makes you better. It allows you to raise your standards but every business however similar is unique in many ways. They may be different in the services that they provide, the approach that they use with their customers or how they operate on a daily basis and obviously there are many more reasons beside these.

When you consider looking at your competitors, it is like being in a boxing match. You need to assess their strengths, their . weaknesses and look at your own strengths and weaknesses. You should have your own game plan but when you are sparring with them you should avoid their strengths unless you are confident that you are stronger than them in that area, focus on your strengths and take advantage of their area of weakness. You should be alert enough and flexible enough to change your strategy should the need arise.

Remember always that the focus of your business is your business and not the competition. If your competitors are not providing a specific service in their package that is valued and important to the customer, then you can exploit this gap in the market. It becomes important for you to focus on developing this service and exceeding expectations of your customers rather than focusing on what your competitors are doing.

GET IN THE DRIVING SEAT

This is perhaps the most important section in your business planning. If you invest your time and complete this section properly, you will have all the tools and steps needed to bring your vision alive. The added advantage of finishing this section is that you can create a blueprint for your business that somebody else can put together for you.

This section involves doing some home play... if you want to maximise the benefits to your business then it will involve making notes. To help you it may be useful to visit our website, www. yourvehicleforbusinesssuccess.com to look at the case studies that relate to each section and perhaps even download the template to keep all your information in one place.

How to handle the passengers

This section of the exercise will address your strengths and weaknesses and show how you can get the support that you need to create an amazing business. So complete the exercise below.

Exercise 7

Part 1

Business Owner:

Name:

Completing this exercise will give you an insight into your strength and weaknesses. It will highlight to you where you need help to run your business successfully.

Part 2

Passengers – Business partners

This exercise will help you learn about your perception of your business partners, their strengths and weaknesses. How you can help them and what help you would like from them. This exercise is to be completed in a manner that supports the team and care should be taken so that you do not destroy the relationships. The weaknesses should be completed in the style that is constructive and not destructive.

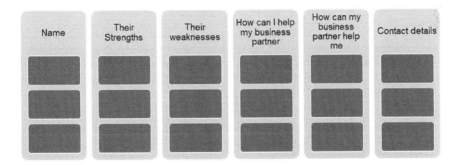

Name	Their Strengths	Their weaknesses	How can I help my business partner	How can my business partner help me	Contact details

This is a very empowering and yet humbling exercise. Here you have made yourself vulnerable yet that could be the very thing that becomes your strength. This is when the team comes together to support one another to focus on the bigger picture and vision.

During this exercise you will have learnt about your perceptions of the strengths and weaknesses of your business partners.

You will have considered helping and supporting your partners in the area of their weakness and ask for help in their areas of strength.

This exercise should be completed by all of the partners and all of your insights should be shared between one another. This will help the partners understand each other and their needs better. You can then agree what help and assistance you will accept and give to each other in the team to grow your business.

Part 3

Passenger – Network

This exercise will help you to identify a whole set of resources that you have. These are people that you may know well and trust or just people you may have come across.

Completing this exercise will help gain leverage by establishing a relationship with them in a manner that will be a win-win situation for everyone.

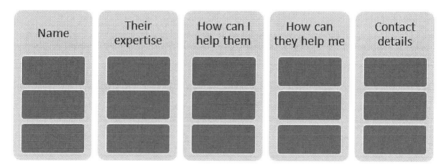

Name	Their expertise	How can I help them	How can they help me	Contact details

This exercise should be completed by all of the partners and all of the lists should be put together to build your network table and database of your business helpers.

Include people that are in business even if that business is un-related to yours.

Include people that have an insight in the business that you are in.

Professionals, for example lawyers, solicitors, business advisors local business development agency and so on

People in a trade, for example builders, electricians, plumbers, architects and so on.

Trusted friends that have always been there to support and help you.

You have just created your database of resources, friends, colleagues and acquaintances that are there to help and assist you in growing your business.

Part 4

Passenger – Customer

This exercise will help you build a profile for your ideal customer and locate them. Once you have identified them, their problem and their solution you just need to go get them.

Ask every partner in the business to do this exercise as each one of them may have a different customer in mind.

Age	
Gender	
Annual income	
Nationality/Ethnicity	
Standard of education	
Geographic location	
Working/Unemployed	
Value of mortgage debt	
Monthly outgoings	
Own home/Rented	
Lives alone/Shares with family/Shares with friends	
Married/ Separated/ Divorced/ Single	
Personality	
Values	
Beliefs	
Attitudes	
Interests	
Lifestyle activity	
Opinions	
Behaviours	
Dreams and goals	
Other factors	

Let's give your ideal customer (profile above) a name. A customer that you may or may not have.

•

Situation

- How do they feel about their life and the world in general? What goes in their life; what are they up to?
- What's their day like?

Problems and challenges

- What's bothering them?
- What gives them sleepless nights – and why?
- List their three main problems.
- Which of these is their biggest problem?

Where do they hang out and where can I find them

•

•

At least 2 Google search results for customer hang outs

•

•

You will have learnt, gained an insight or have a perception of your ideal customer, their lifestyle, their challenges, a solution for them and where to find them. This will help you strategise your marketing material and also shows where to focus your energy in growing your business.

If your partners have defined a different ideal customer to you then if your resources allow, you can get the team to focus on all of the areas and if that is an issue then you can have a priority list. You can start your focus on the one that will give your business the best results when followed accordingly.

How to steer the vehicle in the right direction

Let us review what you have achieved so far since you started to consider going into your own business.

You learnt about your passions and created a vision for your business and understood that there is money to be made.

You have come together as a team or as individuals. Acknowledged your strengths and weaknesses and have a strategy to get help from people around you to realise your vision. This is very intense and can be an overwhelming process. Now that you have come through it, it will be extremely rewarding. You deserve a lot of credit just for getting this far. CONGRATULATIONS. You should celebrate and enjoy your success so far.

You have truly come a long way and yes there is still a long way to go to be where you really want to be. Be assured that you are heading in the right direction. This exercise will help you put things together so that you can successfully continue this journey.

Exercise 8

Now list all the things that need to happen in your business so that you can take from where it is today to where you want it to be.

This list should include only the big steps. For example if you need to make an application for something, here you would simply write 'make application for permission'.

Include any research that needs to take place.

You have made a list of all the things that need doing to establish your business. These are the landmarks of your business progression. As you overcome each of these step you are coming closer to your goals.

If you want to get to your goals faster it is always a good idea to know what it would be like when your goal has been reached. For each of these steps close your eyes for a moment and see in your mind's eye what you would see when you have achieved that goal, what would success feel like at that moment? Enjoy it.

This becomes your reference point for meeting these objectives.

Keeping on the right path

We now have a list of things that need to be fulfilled and a list of people through our business partners and network who can aid us.

The list that was prepared in the previous exercise needs prioritising in order of importance and significance. Each item on the list now needs to be considered individually and broken down in detail. Perhaps with names of the person who will take the responsibility for it and have a deadline for completing the task. You may not be able to give a schedule to everything on the list, which is fine because some of the things can only be dealt with as the business makes progress. To prioritise the list you need to know why each task is important. The efficiency of this plan will help get results quickly because you have prepared for it.

Exercise 9

Part 1

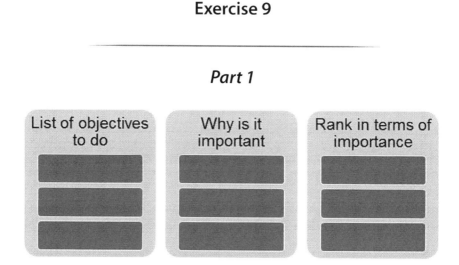

You have now ranked your objectives in terms of importance.

Part 2

Now complete the next task.

List the objectives in their rank. Break down each objective into smaller tasks that need to be carried out to accomplish that task.

Next to each task name the person responsible for completing it.

In the next column you can add the person who can aid or assist in finishing the task and how.

Finally you need to set a time frame in which the task can or should be completed by.

Objective			
Tasks that need to be completed	Responsible Person	Who else can help in the task and how	Expected time to completion

Once this list has been completed, you now have the strategic business action plan. If everything goes to plan, you will have some indication of how long it will take to fulfil your vision. This will also help you calculate how much it will cost to establish your business and whether your current cash flow projection will support it. This is the second checkpoint to assess the viability of your chosen business and should confirm what you had initially calculated in your cash flow calculations during the first priority. Sometimes the two do not meet because during the initial calculations you may have overlooked some of the practical steps and the costs associated with them in establishing your business.

How to buy good tyres and look after them

This is a very important task because when you are recruiting a member of staff for your business and team they need to fit in to your system and be able to share your vision and help you deliver on it.

Before you go about employing someone, you need to have a job description for them and the greater the clarity of the description, the easier it is to find the right candidate for the job.

Once the job description has been ascertained you want to know what values are important for each of those roles.

When you are interviewing your candidates you find out what is important to them in their career and in their job.

The best candidate for the job is the one whose values match that of the values needed to do the job. This obviously needs to be backed up with relevant references from previous employers and friends and their experience, CV and qualifications.

Exercise 10

Job Description	What values needed to do that job well	Candidate values for their career	Candidate qualification CV & reference

You now have a method for recruiting an appropriate member for your business.

Doesn't my car look beautiful?

How do I create my brand? Your brand has to attract the customers that you want. It reflects your values, your promise and your business.

You can build your brand based on your values, your vision and your ideal customer. You now know your vision for your business and what is important to you in business and the market that you are trying to attract to your business. This promise will show up in the service you give to your customers and the standard of your premises.

Exercise 11

Complete the next set of questions and you will form the base of your brand.

As you grow your business, although the theme may stay the same, your brand will continue to evolve.

- Based on your vision and values what experience do you want your customers to have?

- What heart and mind space do you want your customers to have for your business?

- What would need to happen for your customers to experience the above?

- If you had to visualise this brand what would it look like?

- If you had to feel this brand, what would it feel like?

- What noises would your brand make?

- What would it stand for?

This will help you to get started on your business branding. In time you should consult a branding expert to help with this. Only you can decide when you should schedule this.

Take the foot off the brakes whilst driving

Who would be stupid enough to have their foot on the brakes constantly whilst driving?

In business these are the challenges that we are faced with on a day-to-day basis. Some of these are very basic but others are a lot more challenging. We need to be prepared for as many of these as possible so that we are not met with nasty surprises.

To do this well, go through each objective in your strategic business action plan and make a note of all the things that can go wrong. Also do this for anything else that can become challenging in your business.

Once you have identified the possible challenges then you can think about how you can address the matter in the event of it coming true. You can also fill in what help you are likely to need and who can provide that for you. I call this the combat plan.

Exercise 12

Complete the table below.

Challenges	Likely solution or action plan	What help is necessary?	Who can pro- vide it?

You have created a combat plan that will help address any challenges that may occur in your business. This plan will define for you and your team what action to take when something does not go according to plan and who may be able to help and assist you in your time of need.

How can I make the most of the images in the mirror of my vehicle?

You must understand that competition is good for business. Having a monopoly may be of benefit to you for a short time but moving forward it could mean that you become complacent in the service that you provide and unless your business is an essential service you may end up losing demand for whatever it is that you are in business for.

Besides there are very few areas of business where you are able to monopolise in today's world.

Exercise 13

Part 1

Answer the questions below and fill out the table in part 2 of the exercise to address your competition.

What are the strengths in my business?

What are the weaknesses in my business?

Part 2

Who are my competitors?	What are their strengths?	What are their weaknesses?	Where are the gaps in their service and how can I take advantage of this?

You have now addressed your competition. This strategy will help you to keep an eye them and also take advantage of their weakness. This will help you focus on your business and you will not be surprised by your competition either.

IS IT TIME TO TAKE MY CAR FOR A SPIN?

Wow! The second priority may seem very intense and in parts it is still very theoretical. However; if you are passionate about your business then all of this, although appears to be demanding, is simply about implementing your mighty action plan (map) for your business. It is the map that your business will follow to achieve its greatness.

Before you start to take a ride in your vehicle you need to have achieved the following:

You have gained an insight into your personal strengths and weaknesses with respect to your business. This has allowed you to appreciate the help and support that you would like in making it successful.

You have achieved an understanding of your business partners' strengths and weaknesses. This has allowed you to support one another in their areas of vulnerability and focus on your strengths to fulfil your team's business vision.

You have identified how your business partner/s can be resourceful for the business.

You have created your Network table, a database of resources from your friends, colleagues and acquaintances that are there to help and assist you in growing your business.

You have identified and created a profile of your ideal customer. This will allow you to understand their challenges and problems.

You have also established where they are likely to be found. This insight will allow you to go to where your ideal customers hang out and be able to sell your solution package for their ailments.

You have made a list of objectives that needs to be completed to establish your business. These are the landmarks of your business progression. As you overcome each of these step you are coming closer to your goals.

You have ranked your objectives in terms of importance.

You have defined your strategic business action plan. These are the detailed steps that will deliver each of the objectives in your business, focusing your energies in driving your business in the right direction.

You have established a method for employing the most appropriate candidate for your business. This will take into account the job role and the candidate's ability to deliver the expectations in that position.

You have taken huge steps in creating your business branding. This will give you great positioning in the minds of your customer and can only support and aid the prosperity of your business.

You have created a combat plan that will help address any challenges that may occur in your business. This plan will define for you and your team what action to take when something does not go according to plan and who may be able to help and assist you in your time of need.

You have now addressed your competition. This strategy will help you to keep an eye them and also take advantage of their weaknesses. This will help you focus on your business and you will not be caught unawares by your competitors.

Completing the second priority will create the blueprint for your business success. Although this can be a very intense process it is broken down in a systemic manner into bite size chunks. This allows you to deal with each aspect of your business in manner that is not overwhelming or tedious.

This priority completes all of the theoretical aspect of your business and formulates for you the practical processes that need to be undertaken for a thriving and a successful future.

To further assist your progress in your business you can download the template for 'your vehicle for business success' from our website *www.yourvehicleforbusinesssuccess.com.*

This template will allow you to keep current with your plan and as you grow you can revisit each step and make all the necessary changes that come with success.

You will also find on that website real life examples of businesses that have used the template so that it will assist you in completing each exercise.

All the things that have been addressed in this priority are not often done by many business owners. A lot of business owners jump into their business and become so involved in their business that they do not have the time to work on it. Many new or potential business owners never work on their business because they simply do not know how to begin.

CONGRATULATIONS, you have now truly started to take a spin in your business vehicle. Your journey has begun and your preparations for that trip will ensure that it is easy and prosperous.

5

ACCELLERATE TO YOUR BUSINESS SUCCESS-THE THIRD PRIORITY.

WHY DO I WANT TO ACCELERATE MY BUSINESS SUCCESS?

Your amazing drive has truly begun. You have taken your vehicle for a spin and you are in the driving seat. The car is picking up speed and you have a strategy for your journey.

Great journeys begin with the first step and if you have followed the plan thus far you will have come a very long way already. The third priority deals with what to look out for in your business and what actions to take or avoid to ensure that you stay on the right path and then speed up. Often it is not the big dramatic steps that give the most success in business but the small subtle ones.

This priority will look at the importance of the daily performance of your business so that you can focus your energies, on a day-to-day basis in areas that make your business efficient and profitable. It will help you review your business in a manner that will look at the progress made on this journey, how you can increase profit in your business without making any extra sales, the aspect of marketing and your annual accounts.

Why do I have to have a dashboard (daily report)?

The daily report gives you a quick overview of how the day has been for you in your business. Just like the dashboard in your car, when you switch on the engine, you will look to see if any warning lights have come on. If whilst you are driving you see a light go on, you will notice it immediately and take relevant action. Once you start to implement doing the daily report then it will be something that your team will continue when you are absent from the business. Sometimes resistance can set in because your staff and business partners may feel that they are not being trusted and this can affect the relationship between all those that are involved. Therefore it is important to lead by example and get the buy in from everyone to give this process a great chance of success.

When the daily report is done correctly and followed up regularly, it will allow you to keep an eye on your business when you are not there. Going forward it will mean that you while you concentrate on working *on* the business you will be able to know what is happening *in* the business on a daily basis.

Your employees know that they are accountable for what is happening in the business. This accountability is being measured by the business performance on a day-to-day basis. They realise that if their performance begins to become slack, you will know very quickly about it and so they will continue to work in a manner that is consistent and in accordance to the needs of the business.

If there is a day when business has been extremely good or outstanding, you can immediately chase up what the reasons were for the improved result. This can be replicated in the future and you can hope for continued increased sales in your business. On the other hand if there was a day where sales or performance was poor then you can immediately investigate the reason for this. If the reason was legitimate, for example the weather was poor, then you know that this is an anomalous day. However, if the cause was something entirely different then you can take instantaneous action, which will enable you to avoid those things that affect the running of the business.

Since rebuilding my pharmacy in 2009, I had been looking to recruit a pharmacist to work in the business with me. For two years I had managed to employ several pharmacists that were good but not great. They worked hard and managed to get the work done but by the end of the day the whole team would feel as though they had just been through a war zone. Morale in the team was now being affected. By chance, I had to take a couple of days off at the same time as the main pharmacist. I had a locum pharmacist step in for those two days. When I saw the daily figures for day one, I was astounded and day two was even better. I thought that the staff would have been even more pressured and in a very low spirits. On day three I went in and took each member of my staff aside and asked them how the previous days had been. Each one of them was very happy, they said that the workload was well organised and managed extremely well and they were very surprised that they had achieved as much success and dispensed as much as they had. To put things into perspective, on average we would dispense between 300 to 400 items per day with our usual pharmacists and there would be chaos. On day one we had dispensed almost 500 items and on day two we had surpassed it by dispensing more than 550 items without the team even breaking sweat. I immediately went about recruiting this pharmacist for my business. We agreed a salary that was 25 per cent more than the other pharmacists were being paid, which was the going market rate, and three years on he is still with us. Our business has since gone up by 25 per cent, the team is much happier and I am able to focus on other aspect of my business whilst this pharmacist continues to work on running the business on a day-to-day basis. I was only able to make that decision of recruiting him to my team when I realised his potential from those two days that he worked as a locum in the pharmacy from the daily reports.

How cool would it be if the dashboard in your car had a thumbs up sign every time your car was performing very well or you had put in the fuel that made your car run more smoothly? If that was visible then I am sure you too would continue to take that action to continue and maintain the performance of your car.

Are the indicators indicating in the right direction?

I have likened the indicators to performance indicators or the bookkeeping in the business. If you are not keeping on top of the payments that you should have received you will find that your cash flow will be affected and this will in turn create unnecessary pressure on your business.

Often you will deliver goods or give a service to your customer before being paid. It is important that we then receive the payment and that it is correct. If that payment is not received then not only have you lost out on that payment but if that customer was to come back again, what will you do? And if you do not even know that the first payment has not been paid then it is very likely that you will continue providing the service and not be rewarded for it.

In the pharmacy business, there are many services that were commissioned by the previous local health authority and many times we had delivered a service to them and claimed payments for it. These claims were sometimes not paid at all or only partly

THE THIRD PRIORITY |111

paid. It then took a lot of chasing and catching the right person at the right time before eventually being paid

It is essential that you receive credit for goods and things that may have been missing or returned to your wholesaler or service provider. This credit note needs to be used or show up on your bank statement or on your monthly statement from your wholesaler. I lost thousands of pounds once in my business. I was getting goods from an essential wholesaler that I had to do business with to keep my venture running and they were going through a transition period where they were centralising their operations. During this period their service became extremely poor and we were missing orders, they were sending incorrect items, duplicating orders and so much more. I chased up the credits for my goods and was asked to be patient and I was. They eventually sent me credit notes that did not appear on my monthly statements, sometimes the credits that I was given were incorrect because there may have been three items that were returned and credit would be received for only two of them. Sometimes no credits were received at all. Having put up with this turmoil for six months, I found an alternative wholesaler. When I asked for the missing credits to be honoured I was told that all credit issues should have been sorted within three days of claiming them. It is now not possible for them to track the missing goods and invoices and that they would not be able to reimburse me for what I was claiming.

You must ensure that all the monies and cheques that you paid have cleared your account and that your bookkeeping is up to date. There have been times when I have paid my suppliers and they have not allocated the money correctly to my account. This has resulted in them either asking for the money again or asking for the wrong amount on the monthly statement. This means that unless you are totally up to date with your accounts, you will spend time investigating the outstanding amount, repay the amount again or have an issue with that company until the matter is resolved. This may affect your business relationship, which will benefit neither party.

You can use the monthly bookkeeping and performance indicators to predict the end of year profit and speak to your accountant to help you plan effectively for the paying of the end of year tax. If you find that you are running into difficulties then you can access your business partners and your network to see how you can do things differently to turn things around.

All the indications are pointing in the right direction when you negotiate a business deal with well-established companies or even government organizations. However; you do need to ensure that you are being reimbursed correctly and on time. The relationship should support them and you. On my recent trip to the Middle East, I was approached by a company that was supplying goods to a large hospital there to supply them with medicines. This was a great business opportunity but there was only one problem, the hospital had terms to pay within 60 days of the order but it paid them six months in arrears. This meant that the hospital would tie up six months worth of capital from this company. This may not be an issue if the amounts involved were affordable. However; when the sums of money is close to £500k or more, then you need to be confident that you will be paid. Otherwise you may end up financing that company's deal with the hospital. If this company ran out of cash and could no longer afford to pay its creditors, then expect that you may not be paid either.

If your car is indicating one way and you take a turn in the other direction then you can risk a fatal accident. If you use your indicators correctly and wisely then you will move safely and in the right direction.

Why should you service your car and conduct a business review?

You will usually service your car after you have driven it for a certain distance or after a specified time since your last service, usually a year. When you service your car you look out for anything that needs replacing or make a note of something that will need replacing in the near future and you check for the general maintenance of your vehicle. Doing a regular business review is very similar; you make sure that your business is on track, see if anything needs addressing and make plans for the future.

Many business owners are so involved in the day-to-day running of their business that they do not have time to work on their enterprise. They become overwhelmed and do not have time to analyse what is happening in their business and even in their industry. This means that they are not able to look at the bigger picture.

How often have you set goals or made New Year resolutions that have never been achieved? Similarly many business goals and targets are never met. You can create amazing visions and ambitions for your business and unless you make time to assess your progress, those visions will simply be visions and not a reality.

It is essential to conduct a business review so that we can analyse how much progress we have made in our goals and whether we are still on track. We need to look at our vision and our business strategy and decide if we need to continue along the same path or if we need to make changes or adjustments in our plan.

A review will also be very useful even if we are making great progress in our venture because it will allow us to take advantage of new opportunities in the market place. If we do not make time to step back and look for these prospects then they will simply pass us by.

This is the opportunity for accountability and support. If we have decided to undertake a task or asked a member of our team to complete one, then this is the chance to check on progress. If we have business partners or someone to whom we are accountable then the likelihood of completing the task becomes greater. This is because we need to give answers to other people, especially when targets have not been met. Those people to whom tasks have been given are also more likely to accomplish their goals because they know that they will be asked about them. This also creates a platform to ask for help and support from your partners and network in areas where you may be struggling.

Having regular reviews allows you to stay focused on the objectives and outcomes of your business targets. Whatever you focus on grows. This allows your business to be more efficient and enables you to find better ways to improve the results that you are getting.

This gives you the chance to have realistic expectations from yourself, your partners and your team. Sometimes the timeframes that we set to achieve our goals are either too soft or more often very unrealistic and tough. The review will allow you to look at each step in a more practical manner.

If we are on a journey and the road is blocked, we can either end up in the tailback or we can analyse the situation and look for an alternative route to get to our destination quicker. Similarly we are in the driving seat of our business and reviewing our business regularly allows us to be more proactive in our business rather than being reactive.

Why is my car leaking oil – avoidable wastage?

The oil leakages in cars are common and most of the time the problem is minor and easy to fix. Similarly there is a lot of money that is leaking through the business that can be avoided.

Many business owners are looking for new business either through existing customers or new ones yet simply tightening operations in the business and being more efficient can generate a lot of extra income.

You can save money in the business by using your resources more efficiently. This will save you money and make you extra profit because you are making the most of what you have. You may have too many employees for the income that the business generates in that part of the enterprise. By simply making tactical adjustments you can utilise members of staff in much more productive roles in the company.

By addressing costs that can be avoided in your business you are actually improving your operations; some of these mistakes can be ongoing and have cost implications month on month until they are stopped. Many businesses subscribe to a membership or club that they never really use. Even if the cost of is just £10 a month, it is still £120 per year.

Your company may be losing money because they are not correctly checking in orders that are being received. A loss on that order would occur if there were items for which you were charged yet you had not received them. This sort of mistakes can be avoided by simply tightening proce-dures. Hence, you will save money and improve your business practice.

I carried out an exercise with my management team about the leakage in my business. We identified that there were 26 areas of concern where we were losing money. This included things like unnecessary purchase of equipment, poor use of resources, paying penalties because the team had not read the rules of a returns policy with one of the wholesalers, not chasing up missing credits, poor advertising, not looking for the most price-efficient utilities provider and so on. When we analysed the cost of these mistakes to the company it was estimated to be between £15k and £50k. If we became super efficient we could save in excess of £50k. This was a real eye opener that by simply having better procedures and working more efficiently we could save anything from £15k to £50k in our business every year with no extra sales being generated. All of this would be extra profit as this is simply saving money that would otherwise have been lost due to poor practice. By improving our performance, not only would we save that sort of money in that year but in every subsequent years thereafter.

Why do I have to watch my speed? – Growth rate in my business

If you are driving too fast and fail to control your car, it is possible that you could have an accident. Similarly monitoring the growth of your business is very important.

You need to watch the growth of your business because it will help you assess whether it is meeting your expectations or not. It will give you an indication of whether it is following your business strategy direction.

Sometimes you do not anticipate the success of your business model and the growth is very rapid but you are not prepared. You have bitten off more than you can chew. This may result in disappointed customers and affect your reputation and brand. This sort of damage can be very hard to recover from.

There may be times when your business starts to slow down and it starts to take a downward turn. If you are keeping an eye on your business growth this trend will not take you by surprise and during your review and strategising you can make adjustments to your plans to support your business.

You will also find that when your business starts to plateau you can become innovative or simply devise new ways of working that will reenergise your business. You will always need time for your business to settle and then you are ready to make the next advancement.

Your observations and monitoring of the areas in your business that are growing the fastest, will allow you to take advantage of this by focusing on these departments. This might be just an opportunistic moment because of either the circumstances or season, for example the Olympic Games coming to London was an opportunity for some businesses to make a lot of money. If a business realises that this is working well for them, they can strategically concentrate their focus on it for that period and then go back to their usual business once the hype is over.

When you see that your business is doing well, you get a buzz and motivation to take it to the next level. It is a great feeling and you can appreciate the success of your achievements. Taking time out to celebrate this accomplishment is always a great way to keep you motivated and adds momentum for future success. Hence, winning and being successful in business becomes a habit and not a one hit wonder.

Why should I change gears – Use marketing?

Changing gears correctly is like using marketing in your business effectively. Just as the change of gears can accelerate your vehicle, clever marketing strategies will turbo boost your business.

Effective marketing is essential for every business but many small-to medium-size enterprises never use this tool to any good effect. Marketing in business is a subject that can stand alone in its own right.

In today's reality where all businesses face stiff competition from large multiples to distant online retailers it is essential that not only do you find new customers but retain your existing ones too. Effective marketing strategies will help you retain existing customers, get more customers referred to you and build a successful business.

Just as important as knowing when to market is knowing when not to market. If we are not fully prepared to offer the service or sell the product then we should not be shouting about it because it will affect our reputation and failure to deliver can cripple our business.

Everyone has heard about marketing and yet many do not fully understand it. Many business owners that I have spoken to tell me that advertising is a waste of money. I cannot agree more because I have been guilty of that. I have spent thousands of pounds advertising my business in areas that have not served me. Those campaigns have been so bad that I could not even think about breaking even, I would have been lucky if I could say that I have recovered 5 per cent of my cost. That was not because the advertising is poor but rather the message that I had been sending was not reaching the correct audience. It may have been that the audience was correct but the media of my message was not or that the area where I was advertising was too far from where I was.

Many business owners set up shop and then expect customers to find them. This might be true for a few customers but for survival and to make a success of your venture you need strategies and ways to make yourself visible to your potential customers.

It is important for us to use whatever means of media that we can to communicate with our existing and potential new customers. This can include social media, newspapers, local TV channels, blogs, websites, word of mouth, YouTube videos, leaflet drops, exhibitions and so on. These are the means that will allow us to remain in contact and continue to build relations with our existing customers, within our locality and business community. The relationships that we establish will become the foundations of our business.

This book is neither a substitute nor a complete guide on marketing. There are thousands if not millions of books that deal with marketing. However later on in this chapter I will share a few outstanding and amazing golden nuggets with you that I have come across through my education and experience in business. I am very confident that even using these tips in their most basic format will be priceless.

Effective marketing means that you become visible to your clients and potential future customer at a cost that will be easily covered by the sales that you make. Not only do you want to recover the cost of investment but use the strategy for continuous and ongoing profit from the customers that you find. If you understand the lifetime value of your customer, you can invest a proportion of the profits into effective marketing strategies that will improve sales and increase your profits.

Why do I have to have an MOT and do the annual P&L in my business?

The MOT on your car checks the health of your vehicle and if all goes well it will mean that you are able to pay the road tax, which allows you the privilege of using the public roads. Similarly the P&L, the profit and loss accounts of your business checks the health of your business and then works out the tax that you owe the Inland Revenue, which then allows you the privilege to continue doing business.

I am sure that after doing business for a period of time you and your business partners, if you have any, will want to know how you are doing in your business. The P&L will show you clearly the profitability of your business.

You can do the P&L at any time and as often as you want in the year, some business owners decide to do it every month, others do it every quarter and most business will have annual P&L accounts. If you carry out the cash flow projections and measurements every month as mentioned in priority one, then the P&L can be done annually to inform you about your profits and losses in the business. Although losses are common when you are establishing your business, if your business continues to make losses then it is unlikely that you will be in business for much longer unless you have unlimited cash to bail you out.

The P&L highlights some very important information, which may help you decide how you focus your energies in your business in the coming year. Based on the profits that you are making it may help you decide upon the pricing structure of goods and services in your business. If your margin has dropped then there may be several reasons for this, one could be that your suppliers may have put up their prices to you but you have not yet passed that onto your customers.

The P&L will allow you to compare how well you have done with previous years in business and this will show you whether you are growing, are at the same place as last year or making less profit then previously. This will help you to reflect on the future of your business.

At the end of your company's financial year if you are efficient in filing your P&L accounts then you can manage your cash flow because you will have worked out how much tax you will need to pay. This will help you plan your payment accordingly.

If you need to raise money through future business partners or financial institutes, they will want to see your business's P&L to verify whether it is a viable proposition for them to invest in.

The balance sheet is the other financial statement that is produced at the same time as the P&L and gives you a picture of the assets in the company. This is important to know because it will inform you of what money has been invested in the company from all of the financiers including yourself, the value of fixed assets items that you are going to keep for a long term, for example your equipment like computers, fixtures and fittings and so on. The balance sheet will advise you what is owed to you. The balance sheet is important to understand because it tells you the value of your company at that given time.

THE TWEAKS

When someone goes to have a facelift, the plastic surgeon will not rip open their face and completely change the way they look; he or she will make small changes that will make an amazing difference to the way that person appears. Similarly, you do not need to make dramatic changes to create impact on your business. This section will look at what things you need to keep an eye on, so that you can make the small tweaks that create massive impact on the success of your business. The advantage of making small tweaks is that it does not change the whole philosophy of the business and so it is more readily accepted by the team and staff that you have. You can get your team to focus on areas of business that are either being neglected or underperforming. Hence by making small adjustment upon the focus of the team may increase performance and profitability. You may inadvertently realise that you are losing business and so you take action to stem that flow of business. Here we will look at what some of those tweaks are.

What is so important about the dashboard, the daily report?

The dashboard is a panel in your car that has warning lights to inform you if there is something wrong with your lights, oil, fuel and so on. The daily report is a table that is filled in every day that informs you how your business has performed on that given day. It should include anything that is measureable and important in your business. The report should include things like number of sales, takings, number of service units sold if you sell services, number of calls/visits made if your business depends on calling or visiting customers. If some of these need following up, then maybe that too can be included.

You should have up to five or 10 measureable parameters that would take about 10 minutes for a dedicated member of the team to fill out and email to the management team and to you, it is advisable to file a hard copy too. Do not forget to put the date on it. For the most important measure you can have an accumulative monthly running total.

The advantage of keeping such records is that you are able to compare the daily figures as well as month on month. It will also give you the opportunity to compare any one month with the same month in the previous years. This comparison is useful to measure your progress.

The report should have space to make quick notes for days when the business has performed outstandingly and for days that have not done so well. This will allow you to take advantage of things that have worked well for you.

We had just opened our second pharmacy branch and on one of the days the takings in the shop had more than doubled. On the daily report I was able to see this and so I chased it up. The team told me that a particular brand of orthopaedic footwear that we had been selling sold well that day. It transpired that we had stocks of these in the shop with many sizes available. Prior to that we used to only have samples in and order the sizes in when customers asked for them. Customers in that area did not want the hassle of ordering the footwear, coming back in to look at them and trying them on to see if they fit. These were customers that had a very busy schedule and if they liked the shoes they wanted to try them on and buy them if the size fit. As a result of knowing this, we now stock up on this brand of footwear whenever they are on promotion. We have also decided to stock all the other products that are on offer and we know will sell. Although, this will affect our outlay of money at first, sales have improved which means that the cash flow is good.

Recently the daily report showed that we had a particularly bad day with our counter sales. It was the first time that this had happened and it would have been an oversight if I had not done anything about it. I called the team together to find out what had happened. The weather had been very bad that day and so people had not ventured out. I wanted to know if that was the case, so I kept an eye on what was happening in the business over the next few days and thankfully everything was soon back to normal. Had the trend continued, we could have taken steps to investigate the matter and deal with it accordingly.

What to look out for when indicating, the performance indicator?

The indicators here refer to the performance indicators in the business which in this case is actually the bookkeeping aspect of the business. This is not to be confused with the key performance indicators (KPI's) that companies set themselves. If you are running your business well then that should be reflected in the cash flow and profit that the business makes. Sometimes we are very good at selling our services but not very good at claiming the money that we have earned and are owed.

This part of the business can be closely linked to the cash flow projection. The cash flow projection is simply looking at the cash flow but this section deals with consolidating your payments, money received for the sales of goods or services that have been made and the banking too.

The performance indicator is the department that keeps on top of your business. It is the check list that you create that you must go through each month to ensure that all of your payments have been received correctly, your credits from your wholesalers and anyone else have been obtained and that all of your ends of the month statements including the bank have been reconciled.

This checklist should also include the amounts that are being claimed and if monies are outstanding or there is a dispute, the person who has been given the responsibility for chasing it and the date by when this action should be completed. When the chasing has been done then the outcome should also be recorded. This is useful because you have a trail of what action has been taken, who you have spoken to and what has been agreed. I am sure that you must have been in a situation where you have discussed and agreed something with someone and then they seem completely oblivious to it when you bring it up later.

If all the payments are being regularly received and you are on top of your finances and other matters in the business then you know that your business is indicating in the right direction.

What needs servicing – Your business review?

We have created this amazing business vision and created lots of steps that we need to take to get to that vision. There are lots of plans and if you have been through this process so far, then you have invested your time and effort working on your business. You need to take time out now to review whether things are going according to those plans. I know that I have often decided to do something, planned it and started it but it never gets completed. This happens because life gets in the way and we do not ever go back to reviewing our plan and never ask ourselves what else needs to happen to complete it. If an action is no longer required we do not have closure on it because we have not signed it off.

The business review is simply looking at where you are in accordance to your strategy direction and then deciding whether you need to complete any further steps in order to complete each stage. At this point you hold yourself and others accountable for the actions that have been taken. If things have gone well and targets achieved or even surpassed, this gives you the opportunity to recognise the good work that has been done and reward those responsible. It is also a time when success should be celebrated to keep the momentum going in your business and the team motivated.

A business review will help you focus on your business and it will also help you to take advantage of new opportunities that may present themselves. Taking your car for a service will sort out any issues that may be hampering your vehicle, and enable you to acknowledge and prepare for any issues or changes that will need to be made in the future.

What is the impact of the oil leaks?

The oil leaks in your business is the money that can be saved if you improve or tighten up the operations in your business and reduce the amount of poor investment in things that does not profit the company.

I am sure that you must have something that you have spent money on that you did not need – well this is what I call avoidable wastage. The avoidable wastage in your business drains your company of cash flow and profit and simply improving the way you run your business would keep the money in the company.

A few simple action steps can improve your net profit significantly and will also enhance the practices within your company. This will make your business more efficient and profitable.

What is my speed?

The time that it takes for you to reach your destination depends on the speed at which you travel. However if you were driving very fast and were stopped by the police or you had an accident it might be that you never reach your destination or eventually much later than you had initially expected.

The speed in your business is the rate at which it grows. This is an important thing to measure because if you are growing too fast then you can plan steps that will support that expansion. If your business growth is slowing down or becoming stagnant then you can engage in activities that will reignite and inspire its further development.

There are several things that you will need to take into consideration when your business is growing very quickly. If things have not been planned then you need to take action fast, otherwise you may become overwhelmed, which may add pressure to the operations of your business and affect your own personal health and wellness. As consequence of this, your business service levels and performance may fall and your customers may lose confidence in you and your business.

When your business speed has come to a plateau after steady growth then you know that your business now has a solid foundation from which you can create the platform for future growth.

When your business speed begins to drop then you know that your venture is slowing down. You need to review the performance of your enterprise and look at why it is that you are now slowing down. Could it be that your team have become complacent, your competition has stepped up a gear in their business or you have fallen behind on the new trends in the market. This is the time to pick up and begin the acceleration in the business.

When we start our enterprise we want to reach the breakeven speed as soon as possible. This is the speed at which your business is breaking even. When you know what this is, you can drive your business to this target. Once you get there your business is stable and you can push on from there.

In your business it is good to grow at a speed but only as fast as you can handle.

What happens if you do not use the gear box – Marketing effectively?

We find customers to make a sale to but instead we should use the sale to retain the customer for life. Marketing is not just advertising but it is about establishing relationships with your customers. Creating that visibility through whatever medium that is necessary is effective marketing. This could be from word of mouth, free publicity for something in the local media, newspaper or local TV, YouTube videos, writing articles for a local magazine or websites, blogging and other ideas. In other words, as defined by marketing expert and author Dan Kennedy, 'marketing is getting the right message to the right people via the right media and methods.'

When you deliver your message in the right way to your prospective customers then you can expect to get good results in your business and growth. The key here is to identify your ideal customer and the best medium in which to communicate with them. You will also need to take into consideration the cost of the marketing plan and whether the budget required to pay for this is going to give a positive return on investment.

To make your marketing a success, you need to know the lifetime value of a customer, preferably your ideal customer. You have defined him/her during priority two. If you manage to connect with them and persuade them to do business with you, then there are two possibilities, the first is that this is a one off sale and that is the end of this relationship. The second is that you have made the sale and retained this customer who has now become a repeat customer of yours. Both of these customers have a value to you and we can call this the lifetime value of a customer. In the first instance the lifetime value of the customer would be the profit that you made from that one sale. In the second instance the lifetime value of a customer would be the profit made in the initial sale plus all the repeat sales that you are likely to make. You need to work out what the customer *is* worth to you and what they *can be* worth to you. If your ideal customer spends £50 in your business every month then they are worth £600 per year and if each customer was to stay with your business for two years, they are worth £1200. Every customer that you gain in that bracket will earn you £1200 a year. So how much are you prepared to pay to gain their business? This is effective marketing.

There are four ways to increase the total customer value, these are:

- Increase the average amount your customer spends.

- Increase the frequency of repeat purchase.

- Offer existing customers a greater variety of goods and services.

- Get existing customers to bring you their family, friends and people they know as new customers.

Through effective marketing you are able to increase the number of ideal customers that you gain and then you are able to take advantage of them and increase their average customer value. It will be well worth your while investing in this marketing strategy.

What can you expect from the MOT – Your annual P&L?

The MOT is an examination of your vehicle that tells you whether or not it is road worthy. The P&L accounts are in many ways very similar; it is a measure of how successful business has been in its objective of making a profit. All companies are expected to produce annual P&L accounts and keep them. Typically the P&L accounts show the income generated by a business and the cost of generating that income. This can be shown as an equation as

Revenues – Costs = Profits

Simply put it is the income that you have made less whatever it cost you to make it. This is the gross profit.

If we then deduct all of the running costs from the gross profit you will have your net profit.

If your net profit is positive then in that financial year your business has made that much money. If the net figure is a negative then your business has made that much loss in that financial year. You should always get professional help to interpret your accounts.

Sometimes your accounts can show a profit but if you have failed to collect the money from those people that have taken the goods on credit then in reality you will not have made any money until you are fully paid up. If those companies either refuse to pay you or go bankrupt, this will need to be taken into consideration in the following year's accounts by which time it might be too late for your business as you may have debts that you are not able to pay off because your cash flow has been affected. Also great accountants know the secret of making good business show less profit for the purpose of paying taxes. Never underestimate the value of a good accountant. In my early days in business I was operating as a sole trader. I had requested to my then accountant to consider whether I should continue to work as a sole trader or as a limited company. He told me that there was a lot of paperwork involved and he would not recommend that I become a limited company. That year I ended up paying more than £34k in tax. It was shortly after that bruising event that I took on a practice manager who advised me that I should meet up with a chartered accountant friend of his. His fees were slightly more but it was well worth it: he gave me the confidence to become a limited company and he said he would look after everything for me. I changed accountants and the very next year my tax bill had more than halved even though the business showed as much profit as the year before.

The balance sheet is the other important financial statement that you will produce at the same time as your P&L. This is simply what your business owns and what it owes.

The balance sheet is split into three parts:

1. Business assets. What the company owns – for example fixed assets such as fixtures and fittings, computers and other technology, cash, money owed to you and so on.

2. Liabilities. What the company owes, loans, outstanding payments to wholesalers and so on.

3. Equity. Whatever is left in the company when the business has paid off all of the liabilities.

Business assets = Liabilities + Equities

If your business has a positive equity then you know that if you paid off all your debts there would still be money in the company.

It is important for you to understand what is going on in your business and leave the rest to a competent accountant, who is an important member of your team.

HOW TO ACCELERATE TO YOUR BUSINESS SUCCESS

This part of the book looks at making your business efficient and profitable. The tweaks that you make and the things that you look out for and take advantage of will make your business an outstanding success. Completing this section of the book will give you the edge over many other businesses who never even contemplate many of the issues discussed here.

This section involves doing some home play... if you want to maximise the benefits to your business then it will involve making notes. To help you it may be useful to visit our website, www.yourvehicleforbusinesssuccess. com to look at the case studies that relate to each section and perhaps even download the template to keep all your information in one place.

How do I look at the dashboard – Daily report?

This section will help you understand what it is that you need to look for in your business that will give you a picture of your business performance for that day.

In this exercise you need to list all the measureable activity undertaken in the business every day that shows how well you have done. It may include number of sales made, takings for the day, number of calls made to potential clients, number of missed appointments, uptake of services and so on.

You also want a space to make notes of days when performance has either exceeded expectations or fallen way short. This space can be used for anything else that is important that needs to be fed back to the directors or the management team, for example any customer issues or any recommendations.

Exercise 14

Complete the table below to create your daily report.

Date:		
List of daily activities	Figures	Performance analysis Outstanding/good/ average/poor
Special notes:		

From this you will learn how well your business is doing on a daily basis. You are then able to take advantage of days when the business has done outstandingly well and also keep a close eye on things when the business has performed poorly. This will allow quick prompt action that could benefit your business significantly.

How to make the most of your indicators – Your performance indicators?

This will help you deal with whatever it is that you need to do to ensure that you are on top of your business. You need to create a checklist that will show what action needs to be taken and by whom.

Exercise 15

Fill out the tables in Part 1, part 2 and part 3 of the exercise.

Part 1

Sales information

List of activity in the business	Amount expected	Amount received	Date	Any issues/ action taken/ name of the person you spoke to.

Part 2

Purchase Information

Name of supplier	Statement checked	Credit notes received on statement & matched for returned/ missing items	Date payment made	Any issues/ action taken/ contact out-come

Part 3

Miscellaneous checklist

Activity	Yes/No	Date
Bank reconciled		
All payments made		
Credits checked off		
VAT submitted		
PAYE sorted		
Wages sorted		
Any other issues		

You have now completed the performance indicator. If the checklist is completed once a month, you will remain on top of your finances. You will be in a position to know your cash flow, whether your business has been paid correctly or not, any outstanding payments and what is being done about that. You have reconciled the bank, account, which means that you are aware of what payments have left the account and what is still waiting to go out, also if you notice anything unusual happening with your account then you can chase it up immediately.

Get pleasure from servicing your vehicle – The business review

This section will facilitate how you can carry out a business review. In the second priority you carried out the strategy direction and the mighty action plan (MAP) for your business. During the review we are simply checking that we are on track. Checking means that if you find you need help and support in the business you can go out and get it. Or if you need to change the objective of the business, you can do that too.

You have your list of objectives and the date they should be completed by. Now you need to go through that list and make a note of your progress. You should review each step and look at it to see whether it is still a necessary step to take.

This is also the opportunity to see if things need to change.

Exercise 16

You can look at your list of objectives from your strategy direction and assess if you have met the targets that have been set. If there are any issues in meeting those targets you can now revise your plan in a way that will help you achieve them. You then set the date for the next review. When each landmark has been achieved you must celebrate the success.

Whenever you are working on a sub-goal then you should look at that in detail from the MAP.

Also here you should verify whether everything is going according to plan and if there are things that you can take advantage of or if you want to do something differently. You can use this time of reviewing to add it into your future strategy.

Doing this review will have highlighted to you whether you are steering your vehicle in the right direction and whether you are on track to achieve your target. It will highlight to you if you need to take any different action. You can also use this time to take advantage of any new opportunities that may present themselves.

Plug the oil leaks – avoidable wastage

Plugging the oil leak keeps the oil in the engine, like keeping the money in the business. If we can identify all of the expenses in the business that could have been avoided, we would have that as profit.

Exercise 17

Complete the table below.

List all the expenses in the business that could have been avoided in the past 12 months	Cost per month	Cost per year
TOTAL cost of avoidable wastage		

You have now worked out the amount of money that you could potentially save in your business by avoiding these expensive mistakes. Although you may never be able to prevent all the leakages in your business, you can still save significant amounts of money by plugging some of these leaks.

Getting into the right gear – For your marketing

You want to market to your ideal customer through the media that would get them to respond the most, at the ideal time and at a cost that makes it worthwhile for the business. To do this you need to identify your ideal customer, which you have done during the passenger exercise in the second priority. You now need to work out the lifetime value of a customer.

Exercise 18

Answer the following questions to work out the lifetime value of a customer.

- What is your average sale to your ideal customer?

- How often will your ideal customer buy from you? This could be once a week to once a month to once a year depending upon your product and service.

- How long will your ideal customer buy from you before they move on or no longer need your product?

- How many new customers are your ideal customers likely to refer to you?

If you answer the four questions above it will give you a good idea of what your ideal customer is worth to you.

Now you can work out what related events or activities are going on in your business throughout the year. A gift shop owner can look at the calendar and have promotions in line with the trends that happen through the year. In January there are New Year sales, February: valentine's day, March: Mother's Day, June: Father's Day, July and August: wedding season, December: Christmas. You can also take advantage of other religious festivals that take place throughout the year for example Eid, Diwali and so on.

The gift shop owner can plan special promotions and marketing strategies that are cost effective and time appropriate. There are lots of things that you can do with advertising, marketing and promotions. Do not do anything unless it is the right thing to do for the right reasons.

Having an effective marketing campaign will certainly take your business up a gear. It needs to be well planned and worthwhile for your business.

Enjoy driving in the fast lane

This is simply to observe what is happening in your business. To do this effectively you want to first work out what is your breakeven point. Also you want to know from your vision where you want to be and you must realistically assess where you are right now in your business.

Exercise 19

You simply plot a point on a graph each week or month.

The Y axis would be sales and you would add a line to show the following

Breakeven point.

Where you want to be,

When you start to record your business growth, you would mark it with an x on time 0.

On the X axis you plot time ... months or weeks.

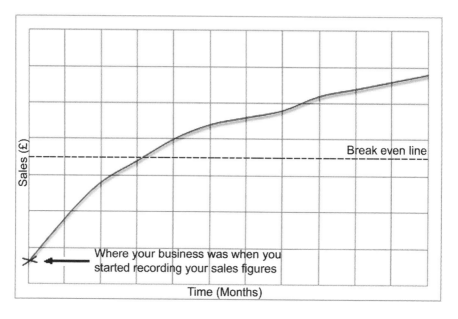

Business trends are sometimes very difficult to spot. It is like watching your children grow up; on a day to day basis you do not really see them grow, yet if a relative has come to visit after some time, they will instantly notice the difference. Similarly, it is hard to notice any trends that are happening in your business, unless you are looking out for them. By observing the changes in your business on a monthly basis you are able to see whether your business is growing, stagnant or slowing down and you can thereby respond according to your business needs.

Taking your vehicle for an MOT – Annual P&L

This is it, the final piece of the jigsaw. When you take the car for an MOT, the mechanic will tell you what needs to be done to your vehicle for it to pass. There may be certain parts that need replacing or repairs required and unless you happen to be a mechanic you do not really need to know the technicalities, only the basics so that you can make the decision as to where you will have them sorted. Similarly, as a businessman/woman you will need to know what is going on in your business but you do need to delve in all the detailed aspects of accounting – leave that for the expert, who can then analyse the results for you. However you do need to know the definitions of what the accountant is telling you so that you can put that information into perspective.

Here I am going to explain some of the basic definitions in the P&L accounts so that you have some understanding of them. I have used arbitrary figures to demonstrate P&L.

Accounts	£
Revenue – turnover, sales income	100,000
Cost of sales also known as cost of goods sold (**COGS**) – this is the cost of manufacturing the item or buying in items to sell them on	50,000
Gross profit – the difference between revenue and cost of sales. This is the profit the business has made before any of the running expenses have been taken into consideration	50,000
OPEX – this is the operational cost or the overheads.	4,800
Salaries	30,000
Advertising	1,000
Administration expense	2,300
Total OPEX	38,100
EBIT – this is the gross profit less OPEX	11,900

EBIT is Earnings Before Interest and Tax. This is the profit that your business has made before paying your tax and any profit or loss you have made due to interest.

Net Earnings (also known as net income) is the EBIT less any interest and tax that you may have to pay.

EBIT	11,900
Interest	0
Tax	2,700
Net earnings	9,200

Through this example the business has made a final profit of £9200. This is a very basic example; In your P&L your accountant will take into account your stock, depreciation of your equipment and amortization which are beyond the scope of this book.

The balance sheet looks at the assets, liabilities and the equity in the business.

Assets	£
Fixed assets – listed by type of item, goods that you will keep for long periods of time for use in the business, for example buildings, computers and so on	50,000
Depreciation – listed as type of item, this is the loss in value of an item. For example if you bought a new computer for £3000 and its life cycle was 3 years then after 3 years it would be worth nothing. Hence it would depreciate by £1000 each year	- 8,000
Total fixed assets	42,000
Current assets – this is the money in the bank, cash. Money owed to you by your customers	12,000
Total assets	54,000

Equity	£
Proprietor's interests – Money introduced by you into your business	10,000
P&L – money/profit retained in the business that was not paid out.	36,000

Liabilities	£
Loans – money borrowed to help the business	4,000
Account payable – money you owe to your suppliers	4,000
Capital at the end of the year	54,000

The total assets should be exactly the same as the capital at the end of the year, hence this is known as the balance sheet. Both sides of the equation should balance.

You now have some basic understanding of the P&L and the balance sheet. You have now passed your MOT and if your objectives have been met through the trading year then you can expect positive net earnings.

SUMMARY AND KEY LEARNING

This priority is crucial if you want to accelerate the growth of your business. Having established what you needed to do in priority two, you now need to address whether your plan is reaping the rewards that you were expecting.

Having been through this priority you will have learned the following:

How you can monitor the progress of your business on a daily basis at a glance.

- This will allow you to take advantage of successful business days by repeating what made those days so good for trade.

- It will also allow you to investigate what has happened in the business if you had a very poor trading day and react accordingly.

The performance indicator will make sure that you are on top of your financial circumstances. It will ensure that the business has received the correct payments and that you have not lost money because of incorrect payments, missing credits and other issues.

Reviewing your business regularly lets you check whether your business is on target for the goals and ambitions that you had when you started your business journey. It will also give you the time to address any other prospects and opportunities that may have presented themselves. Finally, if things have not been going according to your expectations then you can deal with those issues now. You can use this moment to take advantage of your network and gain leverage in your business to meet your objectives otherwise you can make a conscious decision to change the direction and approach of your business.

You will have gained knowledge to run your company a lot more efficiently and thereby make more profit from your existing business. This is achieved by reducing the avoidable and unnecessary expenses that you have been incurring. Not only will you have the immediate benefit of making more profit in your business and provided you maintain the improved level of performance you will continue to benefit from the profits for all the subsequent years in business.

Using your criteria for your ideal customer as described in priority two, you have calculated what their worth to your business is.

Looking at the significant events that happen through the year you can invest in an effective marketing campaign that benefits your business.

Measuring the growth of your business will help you appreciate whether your business is growing in accordance with your expectations or not. This will direct your future strategies during your business review.

You have been given the basic tools to understand the annual P&L and the balance sheet. A healthy looking P&L will ensure that your business has completed another successful year.

This priority is all about observation: what I call the watch and learn process. From your observation of your business you can find areas that are performing well so that you can focus on them. This will allow you to take advantage of this and accelerate the rate of growth of your business.

If you follow these steps, it will ensure that you will accelerate to success in your business.

SUMMARY

All journeys begin with the first step. That step followed by more steps will eventually lead you to your destination. In many cases that first step is simply having an idea, a thought or being forced into doing something because there are no more choices out there. Whatever your situation or wherever you are on that journey, there is nothing better than having clarity, passion, purpose and strategy for that mission. If your passion, purpose and strategy are not exciting or powerful enough to keep you motivated then you may never reach your destination. One in three new businesses fail in their first year.

The journey through this book has taken you through the analogy of the car and how each component of the car represents an aspect of business. This analogy will have helped you appreciate and realise what is involved in running a business. This understanding will help you reduce the chances of you becoming overwhelmed when you are thinking about your business.

When there is so much support out there in the form of easily accessible information and government funding to help people starting out why do so many new businesses fail? There are many reasons for this. Some new business owners do not plan their journey for their business venture. A number of those who do make a plan have a very poor one because they do not have the structure to do them well and may even struggle to understand where they should begin. Sometimes just having a plan without an overall strategy and framework will also result in either failure or a very slow progress because there is a lack of clarity in how the business should grow and develop.

Your framework should inspire you to discover and understand your passions for going into business. This should support your reasons for going into your own business venture. Being passionate about any particular thing does not always make you a living out of it and you need to do your due diligence to ensure that your business is viable.

The drive through this book will have helped you discover your passion and purpose for your business and given you strategies to realise that potential in your business. It will have given you processes that will make it easier for you to work through so that you are able to conclude whether your proposed business venture has a profitable future.

Having your own business means that you must understand the basics. Often that can seem overwhelming and dif-ficult. Simply having a business plan is not enough and you need to be able to understand the basics so that you can use your passion and expertise to create a business that is successful.

The analogy of the vehicle will help you appreciate and understand the basics of business. This understanding will inspire you to appreciate the need for action and when to take it.

The vehicle analogy

Your vehicle for business success analogy will open your eyes to the issues and challenges in business. If you maintained your business in the same manner as a proud vehicle owner looks after his vehicle, you will have a successful business.

It is easy to have a successful business once you understand it. You should now understand the intricacies of running a business without the complications.

Everything does not need to be dealt with at the same time

Yes, there is a lot to know and do in running your own business but the great thing is that we do not need to do all of them at the same time. Just as we maintain our vehicle and tackle each issue at their appropriate time, we can do exactly the same in our business. We must be aware of some things all of the time and how we can do that without becoming overwhelmed.

How do we tackle overwhelm?

Overwhelm happens to us all. So how can the vehicle help us deal with that?

The vehicle has been broken down in to three priorities. Priority one deals with the business owner – their values, passion and vision and the viability of the business, will it make you a living?

Priority two assumes that you have a passion, vision and a viable business and deals with what actions and steps that should to be taken to realise that vision. Priority two will address all the things that should be taken to move your business from concept to realisation.

Priority three looks at the tweaks in your business that will give you massive benefits. We need to know when to take those steps that will improve profits significantly. This priority helps you understand how you are progressing in your business, review your business, checks in on progress towards your vision (are you still on the right path on your journey?) and shows how you can maximise your profit by tightening operations in your practice.

How we begin our journey

You will appreciate why you need to have passion for your business. The exercises will let you identify whether there is any spark in your life for your business.

You will comprehend the significance of your business values and the exercises will help you discover them. In your enterprise you are most satisfied when all of your business values are being met.

You will understand why having a business vision is so important. The exercises will help you create your business vision from your motivation for being in business and your business values.

You will identify the income streams in your business and the potential within your venture.

You will calculate your set up cost for your business.

You will establish the minimum running costs for your business per month.

Using the cash flow calculator you will now know the life expectancy of your business from what you are willing to invest and if you make no sales.

Using the cash flow calculating method, you can work out how much you need to invest to make your business viable.

You can now answer the two questions that a business owner needs to know about their business for it to be successful. The first question is do I have love and passion for my business? The second question is will it make me any money?

IS IT TIME TO TAKE MY CAR FOR A SPIN?

All successful businesses will have a great team. This team is responsible for every aspect of the business from concept to delivery and growth. You will have recognised the significance of this team and your role within it.

You have gained an insight into your personal strengths and weaknesses with respect to your business. This has allowed you to identify the help and support that you would like in making it successful.

This will give you an insight into whether you need to have business partners in your venture or not and what ingredients you need to establish successful partnerships.

You have achieved an understanding of your business partners' strengths and weaknesses and this has allowed you to support one another in areas of vulnerability and focus on strengths to fulfil your team's business vision.

You have understood how your business partner/s can be resourceful for the business.

You have identified and created your database of resources from your friends, colleagues and acquaintances that are there to help and assist you in growing your business.

You have identified and created a profile of your ideal customer. This will allow you to understand their challenges and problems. You have also established where they are likely to be found. This insight will allow you to go to where your ideal customers hang out and sell them your solution package for their ailments.

You have made a list of objectives that need to be completed to establish your business. These are the landmarks of your business progression. As you complete each of these steps you are coming closer to your goals.

You have ranked your objectives in terms of importance.

You have defined your strategic business action plan also known as the massive action plan (MAP). This is your MAP to a successful business. These are the detailed steps that will deliver each of the objectives in your business, focusing your energy in driving your business in the right direction.

You now have an established method for employing the most appropriate candidate for your business. This will take into account the job role and the candidate's ability to deliver the expectations in that position. This will also assist you when you need to employ new staff.

You have an understanding of your business brand and will have taken huge steps in creating your business branding. This will give you great positioning in the hearts and minds of your customer and can only support and aid the prosperity of your business.

You have created a combat plan that will help address any challenges that may occur in your business. This plan will define for you and your team what action to take when something does not go according to plan and help identify who may be able to help and assist you in your time of need.

You have addressed your competition. This strategy will help you to keep an eye on them and this will help you to take advantage of their weaknesses. This will help you focus on your business and you will not be caught unaware.

Completing the second priority will create the blueprint for your business success. Although this can be a very intense process it is broken down in a systematic manner into bite-sized chunks. This allows you to deal with each aspect of your business in a manner that is not overwhelming or tedious.

This priority completes all of the theoretical aspect of your business and formulates for you the practical processes that need to be undertaken for a thriving and a successful future.

To further assist your progress in your business you can download the template for 'your vehicle for business success' from our website *www.yourvehicleforbusinesssuccess.com.*

This template will allow you to keep current with your plan and as you grow you can revisit each step and make all the necessary changes that come with success.

You will also find on that website real life examples of businesses that have used the template which will assist you in completing each exercise.

All the things that have been addressed in this priority are not often done by business owners. A lot of business owners jump into their business and become so involved *in* their business that they do not have the time to work *on* their business. Many new business owners never work on their business because they simply do not know how to begin.

ACCELERATE TO YOUR BUSINESS SUCCESS

This priority is crucial if you want to accelerate the growth of your business. Having established what you needed to do in the second priority, you now need to address whether your plan is reaping the rewards that you were expecting. Through this process you will appreciate some of the most basic things in business that are often overlooked.

Having been through this priority you will have learned the following:

How you can monitor the progress of your business on a daily basis at a glance. This will allow you to take advantage of successful business days by repeating what made those days so good for trade. It will also allow you to investigate what has happened in the business if you had a very poor trading day and react accordingly.

The performance indicator will make sure that your business has received the correct payment so that you have not lost money to missing credits and you are on top of your financial circumstances.

Reviewing your business regularly lets you check whether your business is on target for the goals and ambitions that you had when you started your business journey. It will also give you the time to address any other prospects and opportunities that may have presented themselves. Finally, if things have not been going according to your expectations, you can deal with those issues now. You can use this moment to take advantage of your network and gain leverage in your business to meet your objectives otherwise you can make a conscious decision to change the direction and approach of your business.

You will have gained knowledge to run your company a lot more efficiently and thereby make more profit in the business from your existing business. This is achieved by reducing the avoidable and unnecessary expenses that you have been incurring in your business. Provided you maintain your level of improved performance, you will gain immediate saving and profit in the business as well as ongoing profits in the subsequent years.

Using your criteria for your ideal customer as described in the second priority, you have calculated what their worth to your business is. Looking at the significant events that happen through the year you can invest in an effective marketing campaign that benefits your business.

Measuring the growth of your business will help you appreciate whether your business is growing in accordance with your expectations or not. This will allow you to take appropriate action if necessary, if business is doing well you can keep the momentum going by focussing on the successes that are being achieved. If things are slowing down and business has reached a plateau then you can direct your attentions to other areas of your business that has the potential to grow. If business is starting to decrease and started to decline you can review your strategies and plan a different course of action to take.

You have been given the basic tools to understand the annual P&L and the balance sheet. A healthy looking P&L shows that your business has completed another successful year.

The third priority is all about observation, what I call the watch and learn process. From your observation of your business you can find areas that are performing well so that you can focus on them. This will allow you to take advantage of this and accelerate the rate of growth of your business.

If you follow these steps, it will ensure that you will accelerate to success in your business.

You now possess all of the skills and tools that are necessary to create an outstanding and an amazing business. Use them well so that you can get the result that you want for your life through your business.

THE NEXT STEP

I am sure that you know of people that have learnt some great and useful knowledge but never applied it. However, I am confident that you do not want to be one of them.

YOUR VEHICLE FOR BUSINESS SUCCESS DOWNLOADS

If you have been through these exercises and completed them thoroughly then you will certainly have an amazing business concept that you can fully realise as you make progress on your journey.

Once you have completed these exercises, it is important that you can find them easily without having to trawl through your paperwork and notes. If you are disorganised as I am, then you will never find your notes when you need them.

During a review or at some point you may decide to change your strategy. To record any amendments to the original steps will be very difficult if you have lost your loose paper upon which they were first written or if you have run out of space in your exercise book.

You will want to keep adding notes and tick things off your list as you progress in your business. The record of your business journey should be well organised, easily accessible and allow you to keep a live journal of events and progress.

Everyone knows what a car is. This will establish within your subconscious the connection between each component of the car and its equivalent business analogy.

Keeping records of your drive through your business will allow you to track each step, challenge and success which can become a reference for the future in this venture and others.

You can now download the model, 'your vehicle for business success', by visiting our website *www.yourvehicleforbusinesssuccess. com*. The basic download will help and support you to keep notes electronically. This download will be in the form of the diagram of the car and each component allows you to make relevant notes and record the information that you want. As the files grow you will have a log of your journey in your business. This can become the history or the biography of your business journey. These logs will and can help you set up in your future ventures too.

CASE STUDIES

As mentioned in the introduction, I would like to reiterate that it will be very useful to go through the examples that are provided on our website.

These examples are based on real businesses and will provide a lot of insight by doing the exercises and show how you can benefit your business by completing them well. It will also give you the confidence to do them and see the sort of things that you can expect from the exercises.

You will be able to get access to the case studies when you log on to the website *www.yourvehicleforbusinesssuccess.com* and register to receive them.

JOIN US IN OUR WORKSHOP

Many people invest in books and programs but never do anything with the information that they learn.

I am committed to your success and to help you in your journey I will be running workshops so that you can fully appreciate and get a good understanding of what it takes to run a successful business.

You will gain some very valuable and priceless information that you can easily apply to your business.

The workshops will remove the myth of running a successful business. Getting involved in your own business is daunting and can be very overwhelming. If you can appreciate and understand each of the steps that are involved in having a thriving business then you have already made huge progress in getting to where you want your business to be.

In a boxing ring, how often have you seen one of the fighters beaten even before the first bell has rung? In their heads they have lost the fight because of the personality and perceived ability of their opponent. Similarly many business people are beaten even before they commit to their business and they go into it with a half-hearted approach. Usually the voice in their head is saying, it's OK, I'll give it a go and if it works out great, if not, I'll find something else to do. However their experience in business is so painful and difficult, they often wish that they had never got into it in the first place. This experience leaves them feeling like failures, losers and in a financial mess. They may have wasted lots of their valuable time, it may have affected their families and their relationship with their partners and children. Their social life may also have suffered and after losing their business their confidence may also be affected.

Often you may feel stuck or frustrated in your business because there is a lack of clarity and direction in it. This frustration will show up when you are dealing with your customers and suppliers. You may have a lot of love and passion for the business that you are involved with but when you feel trapped and lacking in confidence you are very unlikely to give your best side in your venture.

The workshop is based on 'your vehicle for business success' and works around the three priorities. You will work on your business idea and will go away with a very thorough framework that will simply need implementing. You will have most of the steps and strategies in place and all you have to decide is when you want to make a go of it.

You will gain an in depth understanding of business and then piece by piece you will put your business framework together. You will go through the exercise and discover your passion and if you have it then how you can apply it into your business. I will take you through a process that will help you discover your innermost business values. Using this and your passion, we will create your business vision together. Once you have clarity and focus for your vision, we will break it down into the big steps, so that you can see what steps are going to be necessary to fulfil your vision, your dream. We will then look at how you can take each step and break it down further into practical process and plan your business journey. You will learn how to create a brand for your business and also create back up plans in case your initial idea or circumstances have changed. The workshop will teach you when you should take on an employee and what qualities to look out for when you are employing someone.

This leads onto the final section and you will be able to learn all of those skills that will help your business truly accelerate to success. In these sessions you be coached on things that you can do that will save the business money and thereby generating immediate profit for your business. Often these are expensive mistakes that are overlooked by many businesses.

You will be shown simple strategies that will help you maximise your profit. It will highlight the things that you should look out for in your business so that you could take immediate action, which when taken will either give you instant success or pick up on things that you can change quickly if they are not serving you.

During the workshop you will be taught how you can do a quick review of your business and the benefits of doing them. Finally if accounts and numbers are not your thing, you will learn the basics so that you can truly understand how well your business has been doing over the year/s.

These workshops will have up to 30 students. You will be taught the theory so that you have a good grounding on the subject. Some examples will be shared to give you a good understanding of how the exercises need to be carried out.

You will be given time to work on your business. There will be times when you will be working in a small group, in pairs and as a class. You will have a safe and supportive environment that will assist you. You have the possibility of coming away with many new contacts that may become part of your network to help you develop your business in the future.

When you have completed the workshop, you will have a complete blueprint for your business. This will take you from being a novice to being a complete professional. Your journey will take you from having a concept for a business through to planning it in detail and then fine tuning it so that you get to your vision quickly and efficiently. You will drive away with a thorough and complete map that will guide you to your business success. All you have to do when you get home is to get into 'your vehicle for business success' and DRIVE!

If you are interested in joining us to plan your business journey then simply come to our website, *www.yourvehicleforbusinesssuccess. com* and register your interest. We will contact you to by email and with details of future events.

TESTIMONIAL

I am Muhammad Morris, My educational background is in psychology and health, I am a holistic therapist, an NLP master practitioner and a psychological coach. I've been fortunate enough to study and mix with many diverse people, I have seen a general trend where most of us have come across people with great ideas, yet the ideas simply remain as such.

This text has made me more conscious and conscientious of wishful thinking and wilful action – as it has provided information I can literally walk with and apply to my business. Rather than simply think and do nothing I sincerely recommend, if you have an idea, sit down, think it through, before you decide to walk away and never plan to do anything with it. Browse through this vehicle of success, because this has the unique ability to make a 2D image have 3D functions. It quite simply for me provides a reality check, gives your product a potential shelf life, which exists out of your mind, and then allows you to know whether your idea is going to be a feasible reality.

Fortunately this business vehicle has provided me with insight and some foresight to make my very personal idea begin to become a practical reality, presently this idea is becoming actualised.

I can say praise to God, I am fortunate to now know what I know, thanks to this text and the exercises that make you process and provide reality checks for things you simply do not and normally would not consider prior to putting your desired business in motion.

Looking at a vehicle from the outside, a car looks nice and flashy, well so does a business idea and dreams to be honest. Thank God the inside of a car has a manual, at least I will know what do with this flashy piece of metal. This sums up my thoughts of *Your Vehicle for Business Success*.

M. Morris

ABOUT THE AUTHOR

Moinuddin Nishar Ahmed Kolia.
BSc(hons), MRPharmS, Certification in NLP and
Results Coaching, Certification in Master NLP and
Master Performance Consultant

Sitting on the embankment on the hard shoulder of the M69 having just hit the central reservation on the motorway, I had this great euphoric feeling of knowing that something amazing was going to happen. It was a glorious summer Saturday in June 1995 and I was returning home from working in Solihull. It had been a very busy week for me as a locum pharmacist and having travelled through the Midlands regularly that week and working some crazy hours, I was extremely tired. Barely able to keep my eyes open, I had considered stopping but as there is no service station on the M69, I continued driving. I was driving at 70 miles an hour and had just passed the road sign that had indicated that the triple lanes were merging into a dual lane in 800m this meant that I was reaching the end of the motorway and into Leicester in less than half a mile. The next thing that I remember was a thud and a jerk, like driving over a hump very fast, the wing mirror breaking. I pulled my car away as it was still in motion and managed to steer it safely onto the hard shoulder. Luckily, I was not injured at all. As I waited for the rescue services to come I was filled with a very powerful euphoric feeling that something fantastic and great was about to happen. So began my journey in business.

The car that I had bought only a week ago was a wreck, the driver's side wing had been smashed, the tyres were punctured and the RAC mechanic informed me that the axle was broken. The car was a write off. Fortunately for me the following Monday I was going to be working as a pharmacist in a store only 10 minutes walking distance from my home. This was perfect because I did not have a car to commute to work. After working there for two weeks, I was offered a job as a pharmacist manager. I would never have considered taking that job had it not been for the accident. For starters it was such a gloomy, narrow place to work, lighting was poor, the fixtures and fittings were very old, the ceiling had chipped wall paper hanging off it, excess stock was put on the top shelf and all in all there was no congruency in my mind of delivering pharmaceutical services from those facilities. The other big issue was the salary, I was being asked to take a reduction in my take home pay of almost £14,000 per year, which is a lot of money now and it was worth even more then and with much greater responsibility.

The owners, Mr Modi and his family were great people and I will always be indebted to them. They put their business up for sale and gave me first refusal. When I gave them an offer for their business, Mr Modi advised me that I was taking a big risk and that the business was making a loss. At the time the business had a turnover of £244k. I thanked him for his advice and jumped into my first business.

My first experience of business was my father's gift and homeware shop. He ran the business for 18 years and eventually decided to close the shop after I had graduated and started working. I will always be eternally grateful for the amazing and outstanding parents that I had. They supported me in every way, including my education but one of the greatest gifts that they gave me was my experience in business. I was allowed to help out on the counter, advise them on things to buy and sell and watch their countless negotiations that they did with their suppliers, not forgetting all the haggling that went on with customers. The two most important things that I had learned from them were that there was no substitute for outstanding customer service and integrity in your business is paramount.

Coming back to recent time, in the last financial year my pharmacy business posted a turnover of £1.3m. In the process of creating this business, I have built the country's first pharmacy and wellbeing centre. We offer a holistic approach to health. We provide alternative therapies, private healthcare and health education events from our conference room. As success breeds success I have been blessed with other ventures that have also been offshoots from this business; we started our second branch in partnership with a few other pharmacists and in our first year of trading we reached a turnover of almost £400k.

I have also developed the wholesaling of medicines within our business. We supply to other pharmacies and wholesalers, we export medicines to the Middle East and Africa, we are about to launch a range of vitamins and food supplement products and our Internet pharmacy business is well on its way to success.

I believe that there is no better way of making a living than having your own business. However; having your own business alone is not enough, too often business owners are working for their business which translates to mean that you end up in a job that pays less, has more responsibilities and requires greater commitment.

I have been blessed and I am very fortunate that I am in a privileged position to be able to make a positive difference to others in business. This model will help you create and grow your business so that it works for you and thereby providing you with greater wealth, more time and the lifestyle that you would like and deserve.

28945858R00106

Made in the USA
Charleston, SC
26 April 2014